MCQs and EMIs
for
MRCPsych PAPER 2

First Edition

MCQs AND EMIs FOR MRCPsych PAPER 2

Dr. Imran S. Malik
BSc, MBBS, MRCPsych
West End Community Mental Health Team
Central and North West London Foundation NHS Trust

Dr. Salman A. Mushtaq
MBBS, MRCPsych, PG Dip Derm
Community Mental Health Team
South Essex University Foundation NHS Trust

Dr. Imran Mushtaq
MBBS, MRCPCH, MRCPsych, DCH,
PG Dip Child Health, PG Dip-CAMH
Specialist-Child and Adolescent Mental Health Service
Milton Keynes Primary Care Trust

INTELLECTUAL SIGNATURE SERIES ©

First edition: April 2009

ISBN- 978-0-9558450-2-4

Notice

For further details contact:
info@intellectualsignature.co.uk

Published by:
Intellectual Signature Ltd
Registered in England and Wales. Reg No: 06489888
11 Adlington Road
Leicester
LE2 4NA
UK

www.intellectualsignature.co.uk

INTELLECTUAL SIGNATURE SERIES ©

Dedication

To our better halves

Ambreen
Sehar &
Uzma

CONTENTS

PREFACE

This book will be a great resource for all trainees in psychiatry preparing for Paper 2 of their professional examinations, plus will serve as a useful study aid to those who wish to update and refresh their knowledge of the core basic sciences relevant to clinical practice.

The MCQ questions are well written and structured and based closely on the curriculum of the Royal College. The authors provide referenced, detailed answers to each question as well as offering some EMI questions and a helpful mock exam. The book concludes with references and suggestions for further reading.

The authors are passionate and committed teachers of clinical psychiatry and this book reflects that: it is more than just a series of practice questions, but rather a study guide that will lead a student into this important area of psychiatry.

Dr Matthew Broome

Associate Clinical Professor of Psychiatry
& Honorary Consultant Psychiatrist in Early Intervention
Health Sciences Research Institute
Warwick Medical School
University of Warwick

January 2009

INTRODUCTION

It was last year, we committed ourselves to help the trainees, combat the challenges of changes in training and the MRCPsych exam format. Early this year we produced a book for Paper 3 which was a huge success and our efforts were greatly appreciated by trainees, for rising to the challenge when nobody else had the courage to take the plunge.

Now, we are back with 'MCQs and EMIs for MRCPsych Paper 2'

So why are we working in reverse order, rather than starting from paper 1?

Is it purely because, we are Psychiatrists?

No, there is more to it.

Frankly, it would have been lot easier for us, as well as therapeutic for our OCD to write books for paper 1, 2 and 3 in that order. But we refused to be dictated by our own convenience and the publisher's preferences. Our aim has always been to respond to the trainees needs and that is exactly what we have done. Last year our survey of trainees informed us that a resource/book for Paper 3 was most needed at that time, due to the dilemma of trainees in transition from the old format to new format of MRCPsych. As a result we produced a comprehensive resource for Paper 3 exam in the form of 'MCQs and EMIs for MRCPsych Paper 3'.

This year in the light of new MRCPsych exam, the most difficult exam was Paper 2, as reported by the trainees and since than we have had overwhelming inquiries and requests for Paper 2 book. Hence we decided to write Paper 2 book before Paper 1, however Paper 1 book will be following soon.

The book is published slightly later than anticipated, purely for the fact that we refused to compromise the content and quality of the book. We had the option of producing a booklet of half the size, with compilation of questions, without any decent explanation and revision material. We are afraid that's just not us.

The aim of Intellectual Signature Series of books is to provide a resource for every paper, which would cover the main syllabus, divided specifically according to the Royal College curriculum. Including, nearly 500 questions in each book to make sure that all major topics are covered with detailed explanations providing comprehensive revision material. It's also our aim to include a mock exam in every book. You'll find all of this in this book.

We hope that once you have got the book in your hand, you'll hardly need to refer to another book to revise the main topics.

Like always, your feedback is our strength

Imran S. Malik,
Salman A. Mushtaq,
Imran Mushtaq,
February 2009

Acknowledgement

We would like to thank Dr Mathew Broome for his support and advice.

Contents for Paper 2 examination

As per website of the Royal College of Psychiatrists following is to be included in the Paper 2 written examination.

- **Basic statistics and research**

  o Basic study design
  o Basic study interpretation
  o Statistics

- **Neurosciences**

  o Neuroanatomy
  o Neurophysiology
  o Neuropathology
  o Neuroendocrinology
  o Neurochemistry
  o Neuroimaging
  o Developmental neuroscience

- **Advanced psychological processes and treatments**

  o Neuropsychology
  o Personality and personality disorders
  o Developmental psychopathology (including Temper)
  o Therapy models, methods, processes and outcomes (BT, CBT, Family/couples, Interpersonal, Psychoanalytic, Psychoeducation)
  o Treatment adherence
  o Psychosocial influences

- **Genetics**

  o Cellular genetics
  o Molecular genetics
  o Behavioural genetics
  o Endophenotypes
  o Genetic epidemiology
  o Gene – environment interaction

- **Epidemiology**

  - o   Surveys across life span
  - o   Measures

- **Psychopharmacology**

  - o   Pharmacokinetics
  - o   Pharmacodynamics
  - o   Adverse reactions
  - o   Theories of action
  - o   Drug dependence
  - o   New drugs
  - o   Pharmacogenetics

How to maximise your chances

It's normal to feel anxious and at times doubt your abilities as the exam approaches. So if you feel that way, don't worry and just relax. You are not on your own.

Most of the people will find themselves in one of the following categories, near the exam.

Firstly, people who have gone through the major topics in the syllabus and are relatively confident about their knowledge. They need to practice exam-type questions and master the exam technique. For such candidates, this book provides enough questions to practice. All questions are divided into chapters according to the exam syllabus, helping you to assess your strong and weak areas. Detailed explanations are given for all the major topics. So if you don't feel confident about a particular topic, you should read the explanation and notes to revise that topic. In the end you can assess yourself by taking the mock exam under exam conditions, provided in the book.

The other category is of people, who have not had the time to revise the main syllabus and don't feel confident about their knowledge of the subject. Such candidates are advised to read this book from cover to cover, reading the detailed explanations and notes provided. This will enable them to quickly revise all the major topics in the syllabus, while practising exam-type questions. At the end, take the mock exam to assess yourself and than revisit any chapter or topic as required.

Some people are very aware of their difficulty in a particular area, while they are comfortable with other syllabuses. Such candidates can go directly to that chapter - for example Genetics or Neurosciences - and than read the rest of the book as time permits or as they feel necessary.

The book is written with great consideration in mind to help all the trainees, no matter at what stage of preparation they are.

Finally, one common reason people don't do well in exams is because they underestimate their abilities.

You should know your weaknesses but, don't underestimate yourself.

You probably have more potential than you think.

All the best!!

Chapter 1 - Basic statistics and research - questions

1. Surveys:

A. Can distinguish between cause and effect
B. Eliminate bias
C. Identify pattern of disease
D. Are gold standard in research
E. Are not affected by confounders

2. Which one of the following statements about Audits is true?

A. Audits are particularly useful in measuring clinical efficacy
B. Even though a clear distinction can be made between audit and research, strictly speaking both are the same
C. Audit projects generally have control groups
D. Audits are descriptive observational studies
E. Audit is a useful tool for hypothesis testing

3. Case reports:

A. Do not suffer from observation bias
B. Do not suffer from selection bias
C. Can always be repeated
D. Are useful for rare diseases
E. Eliminate chance association

4. Ecological studies:

A. Cannot use historical data
B. Provide information on Population
C. Are analytical
D. Give information on individuals
E. Are experimental studies

5. Qualitative studies:

A. Can study multiple and complex issues
B. Are objective
C. Have no place in social sciences
D. Cannot use information from focus groups

E. Are better than RCTs

6. Which of the following is not an advantage of Case Control study?

A. It's quick
B. It's cheap
C. Good to study rare exposures
D. Good to study rare diseases
E. Good for studying aetiology

7. Which one of the following statements about Cohort study is true?

A. They cannot assess temporal relationships
B. They can only be prospective in design
C. They are descriptive observational studies
D. They are superior to case control studies in reducing information bias
E. Confounding is not a problem

8. Cross-sectional surveys:

A. Are useful for prevalence studies
B. Establish causality
C. Are experimental studies
D. Are free from recall bias
E. Do not need large numbers

9. Which one of the following statements about randomised control trials is true?

A. Intention to treat analysis is not a feature of RCT
B. RCTs are vulnerable to Berkson's bias
C. Mantzel Haenszel procedure is essential for compiling results of an RCT
D. They are relatively less expensive
E. RCTs should not be used to study aetiology due to ethical issues

10. Which one of the following statements regarding Crossover trials is not true?

A. In crossover trials, subjects are their own controls
B. They can be used to study rare disorders
C. They suffer from 'order effects'
D. Washout period is not necessary in crossover trials
E. Carry-over effects is one of the disadvantages of crossover trials

11. Which one of the following statements regarding Pragmatic trials is not true?

A. They are sometimes referred to as 'management trials'
B. They tend to use participants with heterogeneous characteristics
C. They tend to use placebo controls rather than active controls
D. In pragmatic trials, all the patients in one clinical location are included
E. Blinding is difficult to achieve

12. Which one of the following statements about Cluster trials is true?

A. Individuals are randomised to different groups
B. They are useful to establish the efficacy of various services
C. Few clusters are needed to achieve statistical power
D. One of the disadvantages is 'order effects'
E. Cluster trial is not a type of RCT

13. Following are the advantages of systematic reviews, except:

A. Use of explicit methods make the conclusions more reliable and accurate
B. They can reduce the delay between research discoveries and implementation of strategies
C. Systematic review can combine studies mathematically to produce summary of effect
D. They allow large amounts of information to be assimilated
E. They allow results of different studies to be compared to establish generalisability of findings

14. Meta-analysis:

A. Does not suffer from publication bias
B. Provides best available evidence of effectiveness
C. Increases precision

D. Cannot summarise large amounts of information
E. Comes under RCT in hierarchy

15. Which one of the following statements about economic analysis
is not true?

A. Economic analysis uses analytical techniques to define choices in
resource allocation
B. An economic analysis cannot be applied to audit
C. An economic analysis should ideally be based on a RCT or Meta-
analysis that is scientifically valid and pertinent
D. An economic analysis should take into account all direct, indirect
and intangible costs, as well as benefits
E. A sensitivity analysis is crucial for the reliability of an economic
analysis

16. Analytical observational studies:

A. Are for hypothesis generation only
B. Have no control for comparison
C. Include case reports
D. Involve intervention for the experimental group
E. Are suitable for comparison between two groups

17. Which one of the following studies is descriptive observational
study?

A. Case control study
B. Case series
C. Cohort study
D. RCT
E. Phase I clinical trials

18. Experimental studies:

A. Do not involve any intervention
B. Are not a reliable measure of efficacy
C. Cannot be meta-analysed
D. Are suitable for hypothesis generation only
E. Do not always require control groups

19. Which one of the following studies is analytical observational study?

A. A series of case reports describing childhood schizophrenia
B. A study of incidence of autism in Denmark
C. Two groups of patients treated with placebo and citalopram respectively
D. All the patients in a surgery were given flu vaccine and observed for a year to see whether they develop flu or not
E. Two groups of smokers and non-smokers, followed up for 20 years to observe the occurrence of lung cancer in both groups

20. A research finding can be false due to the following reasons, except:

A. Chance
B. Bias
C. Confounding
D. Cause
E. Reverse causality

21. Which one of the following statements about Type I error is true?

A. It is also referred to as false negative
B. It can be defined as 'rejecting the null hypothesis when it is in fact true'
C. It can be defined as 'accepting the null hypothesis when it is in fact false'
D. Generally in a statistical test, the probability of a type I error is equal to the value calculated for beta
E. Bias is not a cause of type I error

22. Which one of the following statements about Type II error is true?

A. It can be defined as 'accepting the null hypothesis when it is true'
B. It is also referred to as false positive
C. It can occur due to small sample size
D. In a statistical test, the probability of a type II error is equal to the value set for alpha
E. It is not associated with large variance

23. Which one of the following statements about bias is true?

A. Bias describes the presence of chance in a study
B. Bias can be measured statistically
C. Bias can be controlled for statistically
D. Bias cannot be reduced by good research techniques
E. Bias can be defined as 'any process at any stage of inference which tends to produce results or conclusions that differ (systematically) from the truth

24. Bias referring to the systematic differences between the comparison groups in the loss of participants from the study is called:

A. Performance bias
B. Attrition bias
C. Response bias
D. Membership bias
E. Admission bias

25. In a case control study, sample population is taken from a hospital setting, which does not reflect the rate or severity of the condition in the population. This could mean that the relationship between exposure and disease is not representative of the real population. This type of bias is called:

A. Hawthorne effect
B. Neyman bias
C. Expectation bias
D. Diagnostic purity bias
E. Berkson bias

26. Subjects in a study may alter their behaviour, if they are aware that they are being observed in a study. This may give rise to a bias called:

A. Hawthorne effect
B. Expectation bias
C. Neyman bias
D. Membership bias
E. Sampling bias

27. The bias arising due to a time gap between exposure and the actual selection of the study population, such that some individuals with the exposure are not available for selection, is called:

A. Recall bias
B. Neyman bias
C. Response bias
D. Ascertainment bias
E. Diagnostic suspicion bias

28. Following statements about bias are true, except:

A. Bias undermines the internal validity of the research
B. Bias undermines the external validity of the research
C. All observational studies have built-in bias
D. Bias in research denotes deviation from the truth
E. Selection bias stems from an absence of comparability between groups being studied

29. Publication bias:

A. Is also known as simple attention bias
B. Is seen in systematic reviews
C. Is common in case control studies
D. Is the same as obsequiousness bias
E. Can be detected by forest plot

30. The following statements about confounding are true, except:

A. A confounder may be associated with the exposure but not the consequence of the exposure
B. A confounder may be associated with the outcome, independently of the exposure
C. A positive confounder results in an association between two variables that are not associated
D. A negative confounder masks an association which is really present
E. A confounder has a linear relationship with both the exposure and the outcome

31. In the presence of more than one variable, once the study has been completed, the most appropriate method for controlling confounders would be:

A. Restriction
B. Matching

C. Stratification
D. Multivariate techniques
E. Randomisation

32. Which one of the following statements regarding reliability is true?

A. Reliability can be calculated with certainty
B. Test-retest reliability and internal consistency are interchangeable terms
C. Reliability can be quantified as a correlation coefficient
D. 0.2 value of kappa suggests significant agreement beyond chance
E. Inter-rater reliability is the same as intra-rater reliability

33. Which one of the following statements about validity is true?

A. Validity describes the consistency of a measure
B. Predictive validity is a type of content validity
C. Criterion validity means appearing valid on superficial consideration
D. Validity refers to the extent to which a test measures what it is supposed to measure
E. Construct validity refers to the extent to which the test measures variables that are related to that which should be measured by the test

34. Which one of the following statements is true regarding intention to treat analysis?

A. Intention to treat analysis reduces confounding
B. All study participants that complete the study are included in the analysis
C. It is a method of analysis for randomised trials in which all patients randomly assigned to one of the treatments are analysed together, whether or not they complete the study or receive that treatment
D. All compliant study participants are included in the study
E. The clinical effectiveness can be underestimated if intention to treat analysis is not used

35. A co-relational study that looks at the whole population of a city

by using social services record base to assess any association between depression and social class is an example of:

A. Cohort study
B. Ecological study
C. Case control study
D. Cross-sectional survey
E. Pragmatic trial

36. In order to assess the local community mental health services, several focus groups are arranged to get feedback from service users regarding specific aspects of the service. The feedback is then analysed to identify the key issues raised by service users. A report is prepared to highlight the issues and recommendations made to address these issues. The type of study is an:

A. Ecological study
B. Cross-sectional survey
C. Audit
D. Economic analysis
E. Qualitative study

37. In order to compare 3 different models of services for running polyclinics, 18 polyclinics in the city are randomised to receive these different service packages, with equal number of groups for each service. This is an example of a:

A. Randomised controlled trial
B. Quasi-randomised trial
C. Cluster trial
D. Pragmatic trial
E. Phase 1 trial

38. You want to assess and compare the effectiveness of 2 interventions for generalised anxiety disorder. You want your study to be more reflective of everyday clinical practice. You also want to minimise bias and confounding by having active controls, and ensuring randomisation and blinding. What would be the most appropriate study design?

A. Randomised controlled trial
B. Controlled trial

C. Factorial RCT
D. Cross-over trial
E. Pragmatic trial

39. Quantitative data:

A. Can only have set values
B. Can be further divided into nominal and ordinal data
C. Cannot be distributed non-normally
D. Is also known as numerical data
E. Cannot be measured on a scale

40. Commonly used statistical tests for non-parametric data include:

A. Mean
B. Median
C. Standard deviation
D. Student's T test
E. ANOVA

41. All the following statements regarding chi-squared test are true, except:

A. Compares 2 or more groups
B. In chi-squared test proportions are not used
C. Compares between the expected values and the actual observed values in a 2x2 table
D. In chi-squared test actual numbers are not used
E. In chi-squared test percentages are not used

42. Which one of the following statements about regression is not true?

A. Regression measures the extent to which one or more explanatory variables predict an outcome variable
B. The regression line cannot be constructed by using the regression equation
C. Regression is used to examine the nature of linear relationship between x and y
D. The regression equation represents how much y changes with change of x
E. Regression equation can be used to construct a scatter diagram

43. Relative risk can be defined as:

A. Risk of an event in one group minus the risk in the other group
B. The risk of an event in one group divided by the risk in the other group
C. The probability that the observed difference between the treatments is due to chance
D. The number of patients required to be treated with the experimental intervention in order to prevent one additional adverse outcome
E. The ratio of odds of having the disorder in the experimental group relative to the odds in favour of having the disorder in the control group

44. Specificity can be defined:

A. It measures the proportion of people with a disorder correctly classified by a test
B. It measures the proportion of people with a positive test result who actually have the disorder
C. It measure the proportion of people without a disorder correctly classified by a test
D. It measures the proportion of people with a negative test who do not have the disorder
E. A ratio of the probability of a positive test coming from someone with the disorder compared to one without the disorder

45. Sensitivity can be calculated by using the following formula:

A. $a/(a + c)$
B. $d/(b + d)$
C. $a/(a + b)$
D. $d/(c + d)$
E. Sensitivity$/(1 - $Specificity$)$

46. Absolute Risk Reduction (ARR) can be calculated by using the following formula:

A. EER/CER
B. (CER-EER)/CER
C. CER-EER
D. 1/ARR
E. $(a/b)/(c/d)$

47. Which one of the following statements about Receiver Operating Characteristic (ROC) curve is true?

A. Traditionally the false positive rate on the plot is shown on the Y axis
B. Traditionally the true positive rate on the plot is shown on the X axis
C. The accuracy of a test is measured by the area under the ROC curve
D. An area of 1 represents a poor diagnostic test
E. An area of 0.5 and less represents an ideal diagnostic test

48. Following statements regarding Survival analysis are true, except:

A. It studies the time between entry into a study and occurrence of an event
B. Originally such analyses were performed to give information on time to death in fatal conditions
C. Unequal observation periods make it difficult to determine the mean survival times
D. It can be applied to data from longitudinal cohort studies
E. In survival analysis, censored observations make it easy to determine the mean survival times

49. Following statements regarding Kaplan-Meier survival analysis are true, except:

A. It looks at event rate over the study period rather than just at a specific time point
B. It is used to determine survival probabilities and proportions of individuals surviving
C. It enables the estimation of a cumulative survival probability
D. Log rank test cannot be used when comparing median survival times
E. Survival curve can take into account censored observations

50. Economic analysis that compares alternatives by using a generic monetary outcome is called:

A. Cost Minimisation analysis
B. Cost Efficacy analysis

C. Cost Effectiveness analysis
D. Cost Utility analysis
E. Cost Benefit analysis

51. Which one of the following statements about 'Funnel plots' is not true?

A. They are also called scatter plots
B. Larger studies tend to lie on the open end of the funnel
C. Smaller studies tend to scatter more widely at the open end of the funnel
D. Asymmetry at the wide end of the funnel suggests the presence of publication bias
E. Funnel plots can evaluate potential sources of heterogeneity

52. Following statements about Galbraith plot are not true, except:

A. Z statistic is usually on the X axis
B. Large studies tend to aggregate near to the origin at the standard normal deviate zero
C. Inverse of standard error is usually on the Y axis
D. Galbraith plot helps identify the studies contributing most to the overall heterogeneity
E. Galbraith plot can evaluate the possibility of publication bias

53. Which one of the following statements regarding 'Forest plots' is not true?

A. Forest plots are graphical representation of results of Meta-analysis
B. Horizontal lines in a forest plot represent individual trials
C. The diamond represents the overall outcome
D. The overall pooled results cannot be displayed as a confidence interval
E. Final result of a forest plot can be produced by using Mantel-Haenszel procedure

Chapter 2 - Basic statistics and research - answers

1. C - Surveys help identify patterns of disease, help plan services and generate hypothesis, providing basis for further research. They cannot eliminate bias or confounders and are vulnerable to both selection and information bias. RCT is considered as the gold standard in research.

2. D - Strictly speaking, audit and research are not the same. The main purpose of research is to find answers to clinical questions; for example, what is the best treatment for a particular disease. On the other hand, audit tends to measure what is actually happening and analyse the quality of the services. Audits are descriptive observational studies, not suitable for hypothesis testing. Control groups are used in analytic studies rather than descriptive studies. Audits are useful in measuring local clinical effectiveness. They are an essential part of clinical governance.

3. D - Case reports are useful for reporting rare diseases and can be used to generate hypothesis. They suffer from different biases and cannot eliminate the possibility of chance association.

4. B - Ecological studies are a special type of surveys, also known as co-relational studies, which study populations rather than individuals, often using databases. They are useful for studying associations between occurrence of disease and suspected causes.

5. A - Qualitative studies can study multiple and complex issues which cannot be analysed by quantitative studies, hence are a very useful tool in social sciences. However, they are subjective and ranked low in the hierarchy of research methods. It mainly involves eliciting opinions and interpreting them by using interviews, focus groups, etc.

   Christine Brown and Keith Lloyd: APT 2001, 7: 350-356.

6. C - Case-control studies are a type of epidemiological study design. They are used to identify factors that may contribute to a condition by comparing a group of patients who have that condition with a group of patients who do not. It's quick,

cheap and good for studying diagnosis and aetiology. It allows studying rare diseases. Its disadvantages are possible bias and confounders and have little statistical power. They are not good for rare exposures and establishing temporal relationships.

7. D – Cohort studies are mainly follow-up (prospective) studies; however, technically retrospective cohorts can be designed. Usually groups of people are followed up to compare exposure and outcome. They are used for Aetiology, Harm and Prognosis. They are useful for rare exposures and multiple outcomes but are expensive, time consuming and unsuitable for rare diseases. They reduce information bias but confounding is a problem.

8. A – Cross-sectional surveys are useful for prevalence studies. They don't establish causality and are vulnerable to bias. They are useful for studying associations but only provide a snapshot in time.

9. E – Randomised controlled trials are considered as the gold standard in research. Their essential features are randomisation, blinding and intention to treat analysis, minimising confounding and bias. They measure efficacy rather than effectiveness. They mainly compare treatments and are not suitable to study aetiology, as you'll need to induce a disease, which is unethical. They are very expensive and time consuming. The Mantzel Haenszel procedure is used to produce the final result of a forest plot. Berkson's bias is seen in case-control studies.

10. D – In cross-over trials all participants receive one form of treatment and then switch to another treatment halfway through the study. The advantages are that they can be used to study the treatment of rare diseases, need less number of subjects and the patients are their own controls (perfect matching). Disadvantages are the order effects, carry-over effects, historical controls and they need washout period.

11. C – A typical Pragmatic trial would include all the patients in a clinical location, which are then randomised to receive particular treatment. They measure effectiveness rather than efficacy and are more reflective of everyday practice. They tend to use active controls and have less restrictive inclusion criteria. 'Blinding' and 'control' are difficult to achieve and dropout rate is usually higher.

Hugh McPherson: Pragmatic clinical trials: Complementary Therapies in Medicine (2004) 12, 136-140.

12. **B** – Cluster trials are a special type of RCT in which groups of individuals are randomised, and interventions are directed at groups, rather than individuals. Usually, a lot of clusters are required to give statistical power to the study, which often is a difficult task. They are useful to establish the efficacy of various services; for example, using different educational programmes at different medical schools and then comparing the results. Order effect is seen in cross-over trials.

13. **C** – Systematic reviews are regarded as the highest level of medical evidence. A systematic review is a summary of research that uses explicit methods to identify a specific question, perform a thorough literature search and appraises studies to identify the valid and applicable evidence by using pre-specified criteria. It often uses meta-analysis to generate the quantitative summary of the evidence. It's the meta-analysis that combines studies mathematically to produce summary of effect. A systematic review does not always use meta-analysis; for example, qualitative systematic reviews.

14. **C** – Meta-analysis combines the results of several studies using statistical techniques and usually complements systematic review. It can summarise large amounts of information and can calculate the pooled estimate of effect of an intervention together with its confidence interval. It allows for assessment of heterogeneity and increases precision of estimates of treatment. It provides best available evidence of efficacy.

15. **B** – Economic analysis is the comparative analysis of alternative courses of action in terms of their costs and benefits. It uses analytical techniques to define choices in resource allocation. Main types of economic analysis are: Cost minimisation analysis, Cost effectiveness analysis, Cost utility analysis, Cost benefit analysis and Cost consequences analysis. An economic analysis is best conducted alongside a RCT; however, it can be applied to an audit.

16. **E**

17. **B**

18. **E** – Most of the experimental studies require control group. However, not all of them have a control group; for example, Open trials.

19. **E** – This is an example of cohort study. A and B are examples of descriptive observational studies. C and D are examples of experimental studies.

20. **D** – There are five possible explanations for any research finding. The first is cause, meaning there is a true association. A false association can be attributable to chance, bias, confounding and reverse causality.

21. **B** – B is the definition of type I error. It is also referred to as 'false positive'. The probability is equal to alpha, not beta. Type I error can arise due to bias and confounding.

22. **C** – Type II error can be defined as 'accepting the null hypothesis when it is in fact false'. It is also referred to as 'false negative'. It can occur due to small sample size and large variance. The probability is equal to the value calculated for beta.

23. **E** – E is the definition of bias. Bias describes the presence of systematic error in a study, which does not occur by chance. Good research technique is the only way to reduce bias, as bias cannot be measured or controlled for statistically.

24. **B** – Patients may drop out of a study because of side effects of the intervention. Excluding these patients from the analysis could result in systematic differences in comparison groups and in an overestimate of the effectiveness of the intervention. Attrition bias can be reduced by intention to treat analysis.

25. **E** – Berkson bias is also called admission bias and arises when sample population is taken from a hospital setting.

26. **A** – Hawthorne effect is a type of observation bias and is also called simple attention bias. People generally tend to normalise their behaviour, which can reduce the true association.

27. **B** – Neyman bias is a type of selection bias, also called incidence-prevalence bias. This is seen in the study of diseases, which are

quickly fatal, transient or sub-clinical.

Grimes, A D: Bias and causal associations in observational research. *Lancet*, Jan 2002, Vol 359, 248-252.

28. **B** – Bias can be defined as any process at any stage of inference, which tends to produce results or conclusions that differ (systematically) from the truth. Bias can come from a number of different sources and should be minimised with on a RCT. Randomisation and blinding are key mechanisms to reduce bias. Most important types of bias are Selection bias, Observation bias, Performance bias, and Attrition bias. Selection bias can be further divided into Sampling bias, which is introduced by the researchers, or Response bias, which is introduced by the study population. Examples of sampling bias include Berkson bias, Diagnostic purity bias, Neyman bias, Membership bias and Historical control bias. Examples of observation bias include Interviewer bias, Recall bias, Response bias and Hawthorne effect. Note that there are several classifications of bias and there can be overlap in terms of types and explanations; for example, response bias and ascertainment bias can be explained under selection bias as well as observation bias. Emphasis should be on the basic understanding and how it affects the results of the research.

29. **B** – "Publication bias occurs when the publication of research results depends on their nature and direction." It can occur when authors are more likely to submit, or editors accept, positive rather than negative or inconclusive results. There is a tendency for those negative or inconclusive results to remain hidden and unpublished. Even a small number of such studies can result in a significant bias. This can distort meta-analysis and systematic review of large numbers of studies. Publication bias can be detected by funnel plot.

30. **E** – A confounder has a triangular relationship with both the exposure and the outcome, but it is not on the causal pathway. A positive confounder can result in an association between two variables that are not associated. A negative confounder can mask an association which really exists. Confounders occur naturally and are not created by mistake by researchers, unlike bias. Confounders must be identified so they can be measured and controlled for.

31. **D** – Several methods are used at different stages of research to reduce or control confounding. Restriction is used at the time of study design, matching and randomisation at the stage of allocation of participants to groups. Once the study is completed, then stratification and multivariate techniques like different regression models can be used. Multivariate techniques are used when there are more than one variable.

    Grimes, A D: Bias and causal associations in observational research. *Lancet*, Jan 2002, Vol 359, 248-252.

32. **C** – Reliability is the "consistency" or "repeatability" of a measure. In terms of tests, it's the consistency of the test results on repeat measurements over time by one or more raters. Reliability cannot be calculated, instead it is estimated. However, it can be quantified as correlation coefficient (kappa, Cronbach's alpha and Intraclass correlation coefficient). A value of 0.7 or more is considered significant for kappa.
    Types of reliability include:

    Inter-rater Reliability: Assesses the degree of agreement between assessments of 2 or more different raters/observers.
    Intra-rater Reliability: Assesses the degree of agreement between assessments by one rater of the same phenomena at different times.
    Test-Retest Reliability: Assesses the consistency of a measure from one time to another.
    Parallel-Forms Reliability: Used to assess the consistency of the results of two tests constructed in the same way from the same content.
    Internal Consistency Reliability: Assesses the consistency of results across items within a test.

33. **D** – D is the definition of validity. Validity has several types. Main types of validity are as follows:

    - Face validity – Simply appearing to be true.
    - Content validity – The extent to which the test measures variables that are related to that which should be measured by the test.
    - Construct validity - The extent to which the test measures a theoretical concept by a specific measuring device or procedure.

- Incremental validity - The extent to which the test provides a significant improvement in addition to the use of other approach.
- Criterion validity - It demonstrates the accuracy of a measure or procedure by comparing it with another measure or procedure that has been demonstrated to be valid. Criterion validity is made up of Predictive validity, Concurrent, Convergent and Discriminant validity.

34. C - In an intention to treat analysis, all study participants are included in the analysis as part of the groups to which they are randomised, regardless of whether they completed the study or not. Excluding patients leads to bias and intention to treat analysis aims to minimise exclusions and hence bias. The groups that generally tend to be excluded are non-compliers, drop-outs, ineligible patients and early deaths. The clinical effectiveness can be overestimated if intention to treat analysis is not used.

35. B

36. E

37. C

38. E - Pragmatic trials are useful for assessing effectiveness and are more reflective of everyday clinical practice. They include all the people in any clinical location.

Hugh McPherson: Pragmatic clinical trials: Complementary Therapies in Medicine (2004) 12, 136-140.

39. D - Types of data can be divided into Categorical and Quantitative. Categorical can only have set values of whole numbers. It cannot be measured and has no numerical value. It can be further divided into Nominal and Ordinal. Quantitative data is also known as numerical data and can be distributed normally and non-normally. It's subdivided into Discrete numerical data and Continuous numerical data. The rest of the statements are true for Categorical data. The type of data is important as it determines the type of statistical test used. Please note that there can be different classifications for data, but the essential types remain the same.

40. B - All the rest are used for parametric data. Mean is the sum of all values divided by the number of values. Median is the central

value, in the middle of all values. Standard deviation is the spread of all observations around the mean, calculated as the square root of the variance.

41. **D** – Chi-squared test is used to compare categorical data from 2 or more groups. In a chi-squared test the expected values and the actual observed values are compared in a two-by-two table. It is carried out on actual number of occurrences and percentages or proportions cannot be used.

    Nikulin, M S, and Greenwood, PE (1996): *A Guide to Chi Squared Testing.* New York: Wiley – Interscience.

42. **B** – Regression analysis is a technique which examines the relation of a dependent variable (response variable) to specified independent variables (explanatory variables). Regression analysis can be used as a descriptive method of data analysis (such as curve fitting) without relying on any assumptions about underlying processes generating the data. Except B, all the above statements are true

    Richard A Berk: *Regression Analysis: A Constructive Critique.* Sage Publications. 2004.

43. **B**

    Relative risk: The risk of an event in one group divided by the risk in the other group.
    Absolute risk: Risk of an event in one group minus the risk in the other group.
    P value: The probability that the observed difference between the treatments is due to chance.
    Odds ratio: The ratio of odds of having the disorder in the experimental group relative to the odds in favour of having the disorder in the control group.
    Number needed to treat (NNT): The number of patients required to be treated with the experimental intervention in order to prevent one additional adverse outcome.

    Semple, D, *et al* (2005): *Oxford Handbook of Psychiatry*

44. **C**

    Sensitivity: It measures the proportion of people with a disorder correctly classified by a test.

Specificity: It measures the proportion of people without a disorder correctly classified by a test.

Positive predictive value: It measures the proportion of people with a positive test result who actually have the disorder.

Negative predictive value: It measures the proportion of people with a negative test that do not have the disorder.

Likelihood ratio for a positive test: A ratio of the probability of a positive test coming from someone with the disorder compared to one without the disorder.

Likelihood ratio for a negative test: The likelihood of having the disease as opposed to not having that disease having tested negative for it.

Semple, D, *et al.* (2005): *Oxford handbook of Psychiatry*

45. A
Sensitivity = $a/(a + c)$.
Specificity = $d/(b + d)$.
Positive Predictive Value (PPV) = $a/(a + b)$.
Negative Predictive Value (NPV) = $d/(c + d)$.
Likelihood Ratio for Positive Test = Sensitivity/(1 – Specificity).
Likelihood Ratio for Negative Test = (1 – Sensitivity)/Specificity.

(a, b, c and d refer to the values in the corresponding columns in a 2 by 2 table.) Further details about calculating these values can be obtained from several books and websites; for example, www. cebm.net

46. C

Relative Risk (RR) = EER/CER
Absolute Risk Reduction (ARR) = CER-EER
Relative Risk Reduction (RRR) = (CER-EER)/CER or ARR/CER
Numbers Needed to Treat (NNT) = 1/ARR
Odds Ratio = $(a/b)/(c/d)$

(CER means Control event rate, EER means Experimental event rate. a, b, c and d refer to the values in the corresponding columns in a 2 by 2 table.) Further details about calculating these values can be obtained from several books and websites; for example. www.cebm.net

47. **C** – A graph of sensitivity against 1 – specificity is called a receiver operating characteristic (ROC) curve. ROC curve allows us to explore the relationship between the sensitivity and specificity of a clinical test for a variety of different cut points, thus allowing the determination of an optimal cut point. The true positive rate is usually shown on the Y axis and false positive rate on the X axis. The accuracy of the test is measured by the area under the curve. An ideal or perfect test has area 1.0, while area 0.5 represents poor test. ROC analysis provides a useful means to assess the diagnostic accuracy of a test and to compare the performance of more than one test for the same outcome.

Bewick, V, *et al.*: Statistics Review 13: Receiver operating characteristic curves. Crit Care 2004; doi: 10.1186/cc3000.

48. **E** – Survival analysis studies the time between entry into a study and a subsequent occurrence of an event. Originally, such analyses were performed to give information on time to death in fatal conditions. They can be applied to many outcomes as well as mortality. It is usually applied to data from longitudinal cohort studies. In survival analysis, censored observations and unequal observation periods are potential problems and make it difficult to determine the mean survival times. In such cases the median survival time is calculated.

Jerald F Lawless: *Statistical Models and Methods for Lifetime Data*, 2nd edition. John Wiley and Sons, Hoboken. 2003.

49. **D** – The log rank test is used when median survival times are compared. The Kaplan-Meier Survival Analysis looks at event rate over the study period instead of just a specific time point. It can determine survival probabilities and proportions of individuals surviving, allowing the estimation of a cumulative survival probability. An important advantage of the Kaplan-Meier curve is that the method can take into account Censored data. Time is plotted on the x axis and survivors at each time point on the y axis.

50. **E** – Economic analysis is the comparative analysis of alternative courses of action in terms of their costs and consequences.

   There are four main types of Economic analysis:

- Cost-minimisation analysis. A cost-minimisation analysis (CMA) compares alternative programs where all relevant outcome measures are equal (i.e., equal effectiveness or equal patient quality of life). It's the most basic form and simply aims to decide the least costly way of achieving the same outcome .
- Cost-effectiveness analysis (CEA) compares alternatives and measures (in natural units) the primary objective(s) of the program (i.e., morbidity reduction, life years saved, functional ability on a scale).
- Cost-utility analysis (CUA) compares alternatives similar as in a CEA, but uses a more generic outcome measured directly on patients; i.e., quality adjusted life years (QALYs), healthy years equivalent (HYEs). This type of analysis is preferred when there are multiple objectives of a program, when quality of life is an important outcome, and when quality of life and quantity of life are both important outcomes. The primary advantage of a CUA is that the outcome measure is more generic, and this is helpful when comparing the relative merit of many different types of health care programs.
- Cost-benefit analysis (CBA), compares alternatives by using a generic monetary outcome (i.e., £). The indications for using CBA are similar as for CUA (i.e., when there are multiple objectives of a program), the main difference being that the subjective judgements regarding the value of health outcomes are made by techniques like willingness-to-pay (WTP) rather than by utilities (QALYs, HYEs).

51. **B** – Funnel plots are used to evaluate the possibility of publication bias as well as to evaluate the potential sources of heterogeneity. In the absence of publication bias, the plot resembles a symmetric funnel. Asymmetry at the wide end of the funnel is due to absence of small negative results (studies), suggesting the presence of publication bias. Larger studies tend to lie on the narrow end of the funnel.

52. **D** – A Galbraith plot is one way of identifying the studies which contribute most to the overall heterogeneity of the results. Z statistic is usually on the Y axis and inverse of standard error on the X axis. In a Galbraith plot, large studies tend to aggregate away from the origin.

53. **D** – Forest plots are graphical representations of results of a meta-analysis. There are usually two columns, with the left-hand column listing the names of the studies and the right-hand column being a plot of the measure of effect (e.g., an odds ratio) for each of these studies represented by a square incorporating confidence intervals represented by horizontal lines. The size of the square represents the weight of the study. The overall analysed measure of effect is plotted as diamond and the overall pooled results can be displayed as confidence interval.

Chapter 3 - Neurosciences - questions

1. Which of the following arteries anastomose to make the Circle of Willis?

A. Internal carotid and external carotid arteries
B. Internal carotid and vertebral arteries
C. External carotid and vertebral arteries
D. Meningeal and radicular arteries
E. Meningeal and internal carotid arteries

2. Which of the following sonography techniques has the highest correlation with MR phase contrast imaging for optimal estimation of cerebral blood flow volume?

A. Color Doppler imaging
B. Power Doppler imaging
C. Blood flow imaging
D. Standard ultrasound imaging
E. High resolution ultrasound

3. Which of the following brain areas does not receive its blood supply from the middle cerebral artery?

A. Corpus striatum
B. Broca's area
C. Wernicke's area
D. Heschl's gyrus
E. Medial aspect of motor strip

4. Blockage of which one of the following arteries can affect the sense of smell and cause cranial nerve damage, as well as visual problems, including visual agnosia, hemianopia and alexia?

A. Posterior cerebral artery
B. Anterior cerebellar artery
C. Inferior cerebellar artery
D. Posterior cerebellar artery
E. Pontine artery

5. Which of the following is true for functions of blood brain barrier?

A. It allows relatively easier access to hydrophilic substances
B. Glucose enters CSF and ECF via AQ1 and AQ4 channels
C. Amino acids enter CSF and ECF via 9 different transport systems
D. Lipophilic substances need a specific transport mechanism to cross the barrier
E. It provides a barrier to all of the brain

6. Which of the following is not part of basal ganglia?
A. Striatum
B. Globus pallidus
C. Subthalamic nucleus
D. Vestibular nucleus
E. Substantia nigra

7. Which of the following is not caused by disorders of basal ganglia?

A. Bradykinesia
B. Dyskinesia
C. Hyperkinesia
D. Rigidity
E. Paralysis

8. A 55-year-old male presents with right-sided in-co-ordination of limbs, nystagmus, intention tremors, dysarthria and ataxia. Which part of his brain is damaged?

A. Right prefrontal cortex
B. Left prefrontal cortex
C. Basal ganglia
D. Right cerebellum
E. Left cerebellum

9. A cerebellar tumour was removed from a 25-year-old female. Which one of the following symptoms is she unlikely to develop?

A. Semantic memory loss
B. Visual-spatial disorganisation
C. Blunting of affect
D. Decreased verbal fluency
E. Agrammatism

10. Which one of the following is true for brain tumours?

A. Oligodendroglia can proliferate to become cerebral lymphoma
B. Most brain tumours are tumours of neurones
C. Glia's capability of replication makes it susceptible to neoplasia
D. Microglia are more susceptible to neurodegenerative changes than to neoplasia
E. Cerebral lymphoma is the most common primary brain tumour

11. Which one of the following is true with regards to the third ventricle's anatomical position?

A. Its lateral walls are formed by corpus callosum
B. It is located between pons
C. It is located between medulla
D. Caudally it becomes continuous with the cerebral aqueduct
E. It communicates with the lateral ventricle via the cerebral aqueduct

12. In which one of the following systems does Thalamus not have any role?

A. Visual
B. Gustatory
C. Olfactory
D. Somatic
E. Auditory

13. In which one of the following areas of hypothalamus is Sexually Dimorphic Nucleus present?

A. Preoptic
B. Tuberomedial
C. Tuberolateral
D. Posteromedial
E. Posterolateral

14. Which one of the following pathways is implicated in Parkinson's disease?

A. Mesocortical
B. Mesolimbic

C. Nigrostriatal
D. Tuberoinfundibular
E. Corticospinal

15. Which one of the following statements is true for pathophysiology of Parkinson's disease?

A. Increase of dopaminergic terminals in putamen
B. Reduced inhibition of globus pallidus interna
C. Decreased inhibitory output from globus pallidus interna to thalamus
D. Increase of dopaminergic terminals in caudate
E. Increased inhibition of substantia nigra pars reticularis

16. Which one of the following statements is true for pathophysiology of Huntington's disease?

A. Decreased GABAergic inhibition of globus pallidus externa
B. Decreased inhibitory output from globus pallidus externa
C. Increased facilitation from subthalamic nucleus to globus pallidus interna
D. Increased inhibitory output from globus pallidus interna
E. Degeneration of GABA neurons mainly in putamen

17. Which one of the following statements is true for serotonin receptors?

A. All 5HT receptors are G-protein coupled
B. All 5HT receptors are ligand-gated cation channels
C. 5HT2c is associated with anxiety and CSF secretion
D. 5HT7 is associated with emesis
E. 5HT5 is associated with sleep, feeding, thermoregulation and anxiety

18. Which one of the following statements is true for the PTEN gene?

A. Its inactivating mutations lead to tumour formation
B. Its main action is through excitation of the phosphoinositide 3-kinase signalling pathway
C. It is the least commonly mutated gene responsible for tumour suppression

D. It is located on chromosome-8
E. Up to 10 different types of its mutations are known to cause Cowden syndrome

19. Which one of the following statements is true for EEG rhythms in relation to level of arousal and relevant frequencies?

A. Gamma (<0.5 hertz) present during coma
B. Theta (4-8 hertz) present during sleep
C. Beta (13-30 hertz) present during drowsiness
D. Delta (0.5-4 hertz) present during mental activity
E. Alpha (8-13 hertz) present during relaxation with eyes closed

20. Which one of the following statements is true with regards to functions of association cortex in each lobe?

A. Temporal association cortex creates spatial map of body in surroundings
B. Parietal association cortex plays a role in motor planning
C. Frontal association cortex facilitates appreciation of self in relation to world
D. Frontal association cortex is involved in object recognition and memory
E. Parietal association cortex plays a role in language and emotions

21. Which one of the following structures is not part of the limbic system?

A. Amygdala
B. Hippocampus
C. Hypothalamus
D. Putamen
E. Cingulate gyrus

22. Activity in which one of the following cortical areas mainly determines experience of emotion?

A. Cingulate gyrus
B. Angular gyrus
C. Precentral gyrus
D. Postcentral gyrus
E. Supramarginal gyrus

23. Which one of the following structures is important in the process of associating a heard name to a seen or felt object?

A. Cingulate gyrus
B. Angular gyrus
C. Dentate gyrus
D. Parahippocampal gyrus
E. Heschl's gyrus

24. Which one of the following symptoms is present in patients with left frontal lobe lesion?

A. Automatism
B. Deja vu
C. Anomia
D. Constructional apraxia
E. Agraphia

25. Which one of the following symptoms is not related to left parietal lobe lesions?

A. Anomia
B. Contralateral hemisensory loss and superior visual field loss
C. Partial seizure
D. Dyscalculia
E. Agraphia

26. Which one of the following statements is true for Gerstmann's syndrome?

A. Finger agnosia is one of the symptoms
B. It is caused by lesions of non-dominant parietal lobe
C. Urinary incontinence is one of the symptoms
D. It is caused by lesions of dominant temporal lobes
E. Anosmia is a common feature

27. Which one of the following statements is not true for lesions of the left temporal lobe?

A. Deja vu
B. Automatism
C. Wernicke's aphasia

D. Ipsilateral superior visual field loss
E. Absences

28. Which one of the following statements is true for occipital lobe lesions?

A. Complex partial seizures may occur
B. Anton's syndrome is implicated in bilateral lesions
C. Ipsilateral homonymous hemianopia is common
D. Formed visual hallucinations are characteristic
E. Paraphasia is usually present

29. Which one of the following syndromes is implicated with corpus callosum damage?

A. Alien Hand syndrome
B. Anton's syndrome
C. Parinaud's syndrome
D. Dandy Walker syndrome
E. Locked-in syndrome

30. Which one of the following brain structures is implicated in Locked-in syndrome?

A. Cerebral cortex
B. Cerebellum
C. Brain stem
D. Thalamus
E. Limbic system

31. Which one of the following statements is not true for hippocampus?

A. Hippocampal sclerosis is the most commonly visible type of tissue damage in temporal lobe epilepsy
B. Connections within hippocampus are unidirectional
C. Perforant pathway is the major afferent connection
D. There is no connection with the hippocampus of the opposite side
E. Hippocampus plays an important role in memory

32. Which one of the following areas is affected in early stages of Alzheimer's disease?

A. Frontal lobe
B. Parietal lobe
C. Hippocampus
D. Hypothalamus
E. Putamen

33. Which one of the following connections of amygdala is an efferent connection?

A. Temporal neocortex
B. Hippocampus
C. Stria terminalis
D. Septum
E. Olfactory cortex

34. Which one of the following is a feature of Kluver-Bucy syndrome?

A. Hypermetamorphosis
B. Hyposexuality
C. Excessive fear
D. Hyporality
E. Aggressiveness

35. Which one of the following areas in the brain is most critical in controlling aggression?

A. Hippocampus
B. Amygdale
C. Cingulated cortex
D. Hypothalamus
E. Prefrontal cortex

Chapter 4 - Neurosciences - answers

1. **B** - The Circle of Willis is formed at the base of the brain by anastomose of internal carotid and vertebral arteries. These arteries are the source of blood supply to the brain. Branches of vertebral artery and segmental vessels supply blood to the spinal cord. Radicular arteries are derived from segmental vessels.

    Crossman & Neary: Introduction and overview. In *Neuroanatomy, an illustrated colour text*. 2nd ed. 2000.

2. **C** - Optimal estimation of cerebral blood-flow volume may be an important indicator for better evaluation of the patients with cerebrovascular disorders. In a study where color Doppler imaging, power Doppler imaging and blood flow imaging was compared with MR phase contrast imaging, flow volumes obtained with blood flow imaging showed the highest correlation with MR phase contrast imaging. B-flow sonography may be a very effective and cost-efficient alternative for MR phase contrast studies for the calculation of cerebral blood flow volume.

    Oktar, *et al.*: Blood flow volume quantification in internal carotid and vertebral arteries: comparison of 3 different ultrasound techniques with phase contrast MR imaging. *AJNR Am J Neuroradiol.* 2006.

3. **E** - Medial cortex including medial aspect of the motor and sensory strips is supplied by anterior cerebral artery. Some parts of the corpus striatum are also supplied by the anterior cerebral artery, whereas most of its blood supply comes from the middle cerebral artery.
    The middle cerebral artery supplies the entire lateral aspect of each hemisphere. Therefore, if a patient has a blockage in the middle cerebral artery, it is probable that he will have aphasia. He will probably also have impaired cognition and corticohyposthesia, or numbness, on the opposite side of the body. Problems with hearing and the sense of smell may also result from damage to this artery because it supplies the lateral surface of the temporal lobe.

    McCaffrey, P: The Neuroscience on the Web Series: CMSD 620 Neuroanatomy of Speech, Swallowing and Language. 2008.

4. **A** - All the arteries listed in the question are branches of the

basilar artery. At the lower border of the pons the two vertebral arteries join together to form the basilar artery or vertebro-basilar artery. The posterior cerebral artery supplies the medial area of the occipital lobes and the inferior aspects of the temporal lobes. It also supplies the midbrain, thalamus and some other subcortical structures.

McCaffrey, P: The Neuroscience on the Web Series: CMSD 620 Neuroanatomy of Speech, Swallowing and Language. 2008.

5. C – The blood-brain barrier (BBB) is composed of high-density cells restricting passage of substances from the bloodstream much more than endothelial cells in capillaries elsewhere in the body. Astrocytic feet surround the endothelial cells of the BBB, providing biochemical support to these cells. BBB restricts the entrance of potentially harmful chemicals from the blood and allows entrance of essential nutrients. Lipid-soluble molecules such as alcohol and caffeine are able to penetrate through the BBB relatively easily. In contrast, water-soluble molecules need specialised transport systems. Water uses AQ1 and AQ4 channels and glucose is transported via GLUT1 proteins.

    Among the 9 proposed transport systems for amino acids transport across BBB, 4 are sodium independent active transport systems and 5 are sodium dependent active transport systems. The sodium independent transport systems include 1) System L; 2) System y+; 3) System T; and 4) System x-. The sodium dependent transport systems include 1) System A; 2) System B0+; 3) System ASC; 4) System ; and 5) System X-.

    The area postrema and the posterior pituitary area are two regions which lack BBB and are collectively called the circumventricular organs. Here the capillaries are fenestrated like those in peripheral tissues.

    Quentin, S: Transport of Glutamate and Other Amino Acids at the Blood Brain Barrier. *Journal of Nutrition*. 130: 1016S-1022S. 2000.

6. D – Basal ganglia are a group of nuclei which are part of the extrapyramidal pathways. They are interconnected with the cerebral cortex, thalamus and brain stem. Anatomically, there are two major subdivisions of basal ganglia: rostral and caudal. The rostral part contains external and internal segments of the globus pallidus and striatum; the latter consists of putamen and caudate nucleus. The caudal part contains subthalamic nucleus

and substantia nigra. Substantia nigra consists of substantia nigra pars compacta, substantia nigra pars reticulate and substantia nigra pars lateralis.

Nolte, J: *The Human Brain: An introduction to its Functional Anatomy* . 5th ed. 2002.

7. **E** - Disorders of the basal ganglia cause abnormal control of posture and body movements; it also leads to changes in muscle tone. It does not, however, cause paralysis or any sensory loss. Examples of basal ganglia disorders include Parkinson's disease and Huntington's disease.

Crossman & Neary: Introduction and overview. In *Neuroanatomy an illustrated colour text*. 2nd ed. 2000.

8. **D** - This is a presentation of cerebellar syndrome. Cerebellum co-ordinates movements of the ipsilateral side of the body.

Manto & Pandolfo: *The Cerebellum and Its Disorders*. New York: Cambridge University Press. 2001.

9. **A** - Cerebellar lesions can lead to 'Cerebellar Cognitive Affective Syndrome'. It is characterised by 1) disturbances of executive function, which includes deficient planning, set-shifting, abstract reasoning, working memory, and decreased verbal fluency; 2) impaired spatial cognition, including visual-spatial disorganisation and impaired visual-spatial memory; 3) personality change characterised by flattening or blunting of affect and disinhibited or inappropriate behaviour; and 4) linguistic difficulties, including dysprosodia, agrammatism and mild anomia.

Schmahmann, J: Neuropsychiatric Practice and Opinion: Disorders of the Cerebellum: Ataxia, Dysmetria of Thought, and the Cerebellar Cognitive Affective Syndrome. *J Neuropsychiatry Clin Neurosci*. 16: 367-378, August 2004.

10. **C** - In contrast to glia, neurons stop replicating after development is complete and are only able to go through repair processes which make them susceptible to neurodegenerative diseases. Neuroglial cells include astrocytes, oligodendroglia and microglia. Astrocytomas, oligodendrogliomas, and oligoastrocytomas, collectively referred to as diffuse gliomas, are the most common primary brain tumours. Microglia is the smallest of the glial cells and most serve as the immune system in the brain. Primary Cerebral Lymphomas arise from microglia or from rare lymphocytes that are present around vessels and in the meninges.

Cerebral Lymphoma is a relatively common brain tumour, hence it can affect anyone; however, immunosuppressed people such as patients with AIDS are more commonly affected.

Ligon, K, *et al.*: The oligodendroglial lineage marker OLIG2 is universally expressed in diffuse gliomas. *Journal of neuropathology and experimental neurology.* vol. 63, no 5, pp. 499-509 [11 page(s) (article)] (48 ref). 2004.

11. **D** – The third ventricle is a midline cavity with lateral walls consisting of thalamus and hypothalamus on either side. At its rostral end it communicates with large 'C'-shaped ventricles on both sides in the cerebral cortex via the interventricular foramen or foramen of Monro. The roof of the third ventricle is formed by pia-epindyma which spans between the two striae medullaris thalami, situated along the dorsomedial border of the thalamus. The third ventricle is continuous caudally with the cerebral aqueduct, which runs through the midbrain. At its caudal end, the aqueduct opens into the fourth ventricle, a larger space in the dorsal pons and medulla. The fourth ventricle narrows caudally to form the central canal of the spinal cord.

Purves, D, *et al.*: The Organization of the Nervous System. In *Neuroscience.* 2nd ed. 2001.

12. **C** – The thalamus is a collection of individual nuclei with separate functions and connections with ipsilateral forebrain structures; it occupies most of the diencephalon. Thalamic nuclei also have interthalamic connections. The thalamus primarily acts as a relay centre between the cerebral cortex and other parts of the central nervous system. It is involved in all functions except olfaction. The lateral geniculate nucleus has connections with the visual cortex, the medial geniculate nucleus has connections with the auditory cortex and the ventral posterolateral and posteromedial nuclei have connections with the somatosensory cortex. The thalamus plays a major role in regulating arousal, the level of awareness, and activity; as its reticular and intralaminar nuclei together with reticular formation form the Reticular Activation System. Therefore, damage to the thalamus can lead to permanent coma.

Percheron, G: "Thalamus". In Paxinos, G, and May, J (eds): *The human nervous system.* 2nd ed. pp. 592-675. 2003.

13. **A** – The hypothalamus is a collection of individual nuclei with separate functions and largely ipsilateral connections with the

forebrain. The sexually dimorphic nucleus (SDN) is a cluster of cells located within the preoptic area of the hypothalamus. The volume of SDN is significantly larger in males than in females, caused mainly by greater cell number and larger cell size, in male SDN. It is thought to be related to sexual behaviours.

The hypothalamus co-ordinates homeostatic mechanisms by regulating the autonomic nervous system through its connections with the brainstem and spinal cord, and acting as an endocrine organ via the pituitary gland. It also controls behaviours such as sexual behaviour, eating behaviour and emotional responses, and in addition also plays a role in memory through its connections with the forebrain, limbic system and olfactory system.

Roselli, C, *et al.*: Volume of a Sexually Dimorphic Nucleus in the Ovine Medial Preoptic Area/Anterior Hypothalamus Varies with Sexual Partner Preference. *Endocrinology* 145 (2): 478-483. 2004.

14. **C** – The mesocortical, mesolimbic, nigrostriatal and tuberoinfundibular pathways are all dopaminergic pathways. The nigrostriatal pathway transmits dopamine from the substantia nigra in the midbrain to the striatum in the subcortical region of the telencephalon; degeneration of this pathway leads to Parkinson's disease. The mesocortical pathway transmits dopamine from the ventral tegmental area in midbrain to the frontal cortex; disruptions in this pathway are implicated in schizophrenia. The mesolimbic pathway transmits dopamine from the ventral tegmental area in midbrain to the nucleus accumbens in the limbic system; recreational drugs have been shown to increase dopamine levels in nucleus accumbens. The tuberoinfundibular pathway transmits dopamine from hypothalamus to the pituitary gland; here dopamine acts as a prolactin-inhibiting hormone, hence inhibiting prolactin release from the anterior pituitary gland.

Greenstein, B: In *Concise Clinical Pharmacology. Idiopathic Parkinson's Disease I: Introduction.* Published by Pharmaceutical Press. 2007.

15. **B** – The degeneration of dopaminergic cells in the substantia nigra pars compacta leads to reduction of dopaminergic terminals in the striatum (putamen and caudate nuclei). Loss of dopamine to the striatum results in less inhibition of the globus pallidus interna and substantia nigra pars reticularis, which leads to increased inhibitory output from the globus pallidus interna and substantia nigra pars reticularis to the thalamus. Over-inhibition of the thalamus produces decreased facilitation to the motor

cortex, which results in delays in the initiation of movements and bradykinesia, which are typical symptoms of Parkinson's disease.

Bonnet & Houeto: Pathophysiology of Parkinson's Disease. *Biomedicine & Pharmacotherapy* 53 (3): 117-121. 1999.

16. A – Bradykinesia in Huntington's disease results from degeneration of the basal ganglia output to the supplementary motor areas concerned with the initiation and maintenance of sequential movements. The degeneration of spiny GABA neurons mainly in caudate nucleus results in reduced GABAergic inhibition of the globus pallidus externa, which increases inhibitory output from the globus pallidus externa to the subthalamic nucleus; this reduces facilitatory output from the subthalamic nucleus to the globus pallidus interna and the substantia nigra pars reticularis. As a result there is less inhibitory output from the globus pallidus interna and the substantia nigra pars reticularis to the thalamus. The lack of inhibitory control of the thalamus on the motor cortex results in unwanted and involuntary movements, namely dyskinesias and chorea. The co-existing hyperkinetic and hypokinetic movement disorders in patients with Huntington's disease probably reflect the involvement of direct and indirect pathways in the basal ganglia-thalamus-cortical motor circuit.

Berardelli, A, *et al.*: Pathophysiology of chorea and bradykinesia in Huntington's disease. *Movement Disorders* 14(3): 398-403. 2001.

17. C – All 5HT receptors are G-protein coupled except 5HT3, which is a ligand-gated cation channel. 5HT3 is implicated in neuronal excitation, anxiety and emesis. All 5HT1 receptors reduce cAMP and modulate sleep, feeding, thermoregulation and anxiety. All 5HT2 receptors increase inositol triphosphate (IP3) and diacylglycerol. 5HT2c is associated with CSF secretion. 5HT4 modulates GI motility by increasing cAMP. Functions of 5HT5, 6 and 7 are not known.

Hoyer, D, *et al.*: International Union of Pharmacology classification of receptors for 5-hydroxytryptamine (Serotonin). *Pharmacol. Rev* 46 (2): 157-203. 1994.

18. A – The PTEN (phosphatase and tensin homologue) gene on chromosome 10 is a tumour suppressor that can inhibit proliferation and migration and controls apoptosis in a number of cell types, mainly through inhibition of the phosphoinositide

3-kinase (PI3K) signalling pathway. Patients carrying inactivating mutations of PTEN show a prevalence to develop tumours that can coincide with neurological defects such as mental retardation, ataxia and seizures. PTEN is the most commonly mutated gene responsible for tumour suppression; up to 100 mutations have been identified as being responsible for Cowden syndrome, which is a rare disorder characterised by multiple non-cancerous, tumour-like growths called hamartomas and an increased risk of developing certain cancers. Signs and symptoms of Cowden syndrome can include macrocephaly; a rare, non-cancerous brain tumour called Lhermitte-Duclos disease; and mental retardation.

Van Diepen & Eickholt: Function of PTEN during the Formation and Maintenance of Neuronal Circuits in the Brain. *Dev. Neurosci* 30: 59-64 (2008).

Pilarski & Eng: Will the real Cowden syndrome please stand up (again)? Expanding mutational and clinical spectra of the PTEN hamartoma tumour syndrome. *J Med Genet* 41 (5): 323-6 (2004).

19. **E** – Gamma is not a recognised waveform of EEG. The four basic rhythms defined by their frequencies include delta (0.5-4 hertz) during sleep, theta (4-8 hertz) during drowsiness, alpha (8-13 hertz) during closed eyes and beta (13-30 hertz) during mental activity.

Stern, J M & Engel, J: *An Atlas of EEG Patterns*. Philadelphia: Lippincott Williams & Wilkins. 2004.

20. **C** – The association cortex functions to produce a meaningful perceptual experience and enables one to interact effectively and support abstract thinking and language. The frontal association cortex plays a role in judgement, personality, foresight, appreciation of self in relation to world and motor planning; hence lesions of this area lead to disinhibition, impulsivity, inappropriate behaviour and deficits in planning. The temporal association cortex is concerned with memory, language, object recognition and emotions; therefore lesions of this area lead to memory difficulties, receptive aphasia and agnosia. The parietal association cortex uses multi-modal information to create a spatial map of body in surroundings; hence lesions to this area may lead to hemispatial neglect, disorientation, inability to read maps and apraxia.

Kandel, E, *et al.*: *Principles of Neural Science*. Mcgraw-Hill Professional. 2000.

21. **D** – The putamen, along with the caudate nucleus, forms the striatum, which is a part of the basal ganglia. The limbic system consists of hippocampus, amygdala, septal nuclei, cingulate gyrus and hypothalamus. The limbic system is responsible for memory, agonistic (defence & attack) behaviour, sexual and reproductive behaviour, maintenance of homeostasis via activation of visceral effector mechanisms, modulation of pituitary hormone release and initiation of feeding and drinking.

LeDoux, J: Emotion Circuits in the Brain. *Annual Review of Neuroscience* 23: 155-184. 2000.

22. **A** – American neurologist James Papez proposed that there is an 'emotion system' lying on the medial wall of the brain that links the cortex with the hypothalamus. This 'emotion system' is referred to as 'Papez circuit'. According to Papez, this circuit includes hippocampus, fornix, mammillary bodies, mammillothalamic tract, anterior thalamic nuclei, genu of internal capsule, cingulate gyrus, cingulum, parahippocampal gyrus, entorhinal cortex, and perforontal pathway. Recent findings suggest that the amygdala, septal nuclei and prefrontal cortex also make part of the Papez circuit.

Papez believed that the experience of emotion was determined by activity in the cingulate cortex and, less directly, other cortical areas. The cingulate cortex projects to the hippocampus and the hippocampus projects to the hypothalamus by way of the bundle of axons called the fornix. Hypothalamic effects reach the cortex via a relay in the anterior thalamic nuclei. In addition to the emotional experience and expression, Papez circuit also plays a role in storing memory.

Bear, M, *et al.:Neuroscience: Exploring the Brain*, 3rd ed. Philadelphia, PA: Lippincott Williams & Wilkins, 568-569. 2007.

23. **B** – Learning of names of objects is facilitated by the fact that the brain is able to readily make associations between two non-limbic stimuli. The angular gyrus is important in the process of associating a heard name to a seen or felt object; it is probably also important for associations in the reverse direction. A name passes through Wernicke's area, then via the angular gyrus arouses association in other parts of the brain. It is probably thus that Wernicke's area attains its essential importance in comprehension, i.e. the arousal of association.

Rosaleen A McCarthy: *Semantic Knowledge and Semantic Representations*. Psychology Press. 1995.

24. E – Patients with left frontal lobe lesion may present with personality changes, Jacksonian seizures, right-sided hemiplegia, Broca's aphasia, abulia, flat affect, akinesia and motor agraphia. Constructional apraxia results from the right frontal lobe lesions. Witzelsucht, a term meaning facetiousness, and moria, a form of euphoria, may also be present in patients with lesions of the right frontal lobe.
Intellect is spared in frontal lobe lesions. Primitive reflexes may appear.

Mesulam, M M: The Human Frontal Lobes: Transcending the Default Mode through Continent Encoding. In D T Stuss and R T Knight: *Principles of Frontal Lobe Function*. Oxford: 8-30. 2002.

25. B – Contralateral hemisensory loss in parietal lobes is usually accompanied by inferior visual field loss. For the right-sided parietal lobe lesions, in addition to the symptoms listed in the question, constructional apraxia is also present.

Avillac, M, Deneve, S, Olivier, E, Pouget, A, Duhamel, J R: Reference frames for representing visual and tactile locations in parietal cortex. *Nat Neurosci*. 8(7): 941-9. 2005.

26. A – Gerstmann's syndrome is caused by lesions of the dominant parietal lobe near the angular gyrus. It consists of finger agnosia, agraphia, dyscalculia and right-left disorientation.

Roux, F, *et al.*: Writing, calculating, and finger recognition of the angular gyrus: a cortical stimulation study of Gerstmann syndrome. *J Neurosurgery* 99: 716-727. 2003.

27. D – In the event where a lesion in the temporal lobe involves Meyer's loop, it results in an upper homonymous quadrantanopia. Complex seizures in temporal lobe lesions may include absence attacks and automatism. They are usually preceded by an aura. The aura may occur as a feeling of deja vu, jamais vu, fear, depersonalisation and euphoria.

Bofarton, J, *et al.*: The field defects of anterior temporal lobectomy: a quantitative reassessment of Meyer's Loop. *Brain* 128 (9): 2123-2133. September 2005.

28. B – Anton syndrome, also known as Anton-Babinski syndrome, is

a form of cortical blindness in which the patient denies the visual impairment. Anton syndrome is caused by bilateral lesion of the occipital lobes, which extends from the primary visual cortex into the visual association cortex. Patients with occipital lobe lesions less frequently present with psychiatric symptoms. They, however, have characteristic visual hallucinations which are simple and unformed, often not more than light flashes. They may also have simple partial seizures and contralateral homonymous hemianopia is common.

Galetovic, D, *et al.*: Bilateral cortical blindness – Anton Syndrome: case report. *Collegium Antropologicom* 29(1). 2005.

29. **A** – Alien-hand syndrome is a phenomena experienced by patients in which an upper limb performs complex motor activities outside of volitional control. It is a rare syndrome occurring due to damage of the corpus callosum.

Scepkowski & Cronin-Golomb: The Alien Hand: Cases, Categorizations, and Anatomical Correlates. *Behavioural and Cognitive Neuroscience Reviews* 2(4), 261-277. 2003.

30. **C** – Locked-in syndrome results from brain-stem lesion which disrupts the voluntary control of movement without abolishing either wakefulness or awareness. It usually is due to bilateral pontine infarction related to the basilar artery thrombosis or bilateral occlusion of paramedian arteries. Occasionally, it can be due to bilateral midbrain infarction. Patients are substantially paralysed but conscious and can communicate using movements of the eyes or eyelids.

Pearce, J: The Locked-in syndrome. *Br Med J (Clin Res Ed)*, 294 (6566): 198-199. 1987.

31. **D** – A pathway is derived from axons that project from the CA3 pyramidal cell layer of the hippocampus to the CA1 pyramidal cell layer. The axons either come from CA3 neurons in the ipsilateral hippocampus or from an equivalent structure in the opposite hemisphere (contralateral). These latter fibres are termed commissural fibres, as they cross from one hemisphere of the brain to the other. This pathway is called Schaffer Collateral/ Associational Commissural Pathway.

MacIver, M B: The Hippocampus. In *Neural Mechanisms of Anaesthesia*. Eds. Antognini, *et al*. Humana Press. 2002.

32. C - Hippocampus, entorhinal cortex and amygdala are the structures affected in early Alzheimer's disease, giving rise to short-term memory problems. Parietal lobe is affected in the moderate stage of the disease, giving rise to dressing apraxia; and frontal lobe is affected in the advanced stage of the disease, resulting in loss of executive functions.

Wenk, G L: Neuropathologic changes in Alzheimer's disease. *J Clin Psychiatry* 64 Suppl 9: 7-10. 2003.

33. C - Amygdala has its afferent connections from the olfactory cortex, septum, brain-stem, hippocampus and temporal neocortex. For efferent connections the centromedial amygdala projects through the stria terminalis primarily to the hypothalamus and through the ventral amygdalofugal tract to the brain-stem, where it can influence hormonal and somatomotor aspects of behaviour and emotional states, e.g. eating, drinking and sex. Projections from the lateral and central amygdala go to the lateral hypothalamus through the ventral amygdalofugal pathway. The basolateral nuclei project to the striatum and receive direct cholinergic input from the basal nucleus of Meynert. The basolateral group also projects to the mediodorsal thalamus, which projects to the prefrontal cortex.

Steriade & Pare: The amygdale. In *Gating in Cerebral Networks*. Cambridge University Press. 2007.

34. A - Kluver-Bucy syndrome follows ablation or lesions of the medial and lateral temporal lobes including amygdala on both sides. Its features include hypermetamorphosis (irresistible impulse to touch objects), hypersexuality, loss of fear, hyperorality with bulimia, prospognosia, visual agnosia, memory deficit and placidity with pet-like compliance.

Hayman, L A, *et al.*: Klüver-Bucy syndrome after selective damage of the amygdala and its cortical connections. *J Neuropsychiatry Clin Neurosci*. 10: 354-358. 1998.

35. D - The hypothalamus and periaqueductal grey matter are most critical in the control of aggression. Other structures include amygdala, hippocampus, septal nuclei, cingulate cortex and prefrontal cortex.
Serotonin has negative correlation with aggression whereas testosterone seems to have positive correlation with aggression, but the latter lacks robust evidence. The neurotransmitter vasopressin causes an increase in aggressive behaviour when

present in large amounts in the anterior hypothalamus.

McElliskem, J: Affective and Predatory Violence: a Bimodal Classification System of Human Aggression and Violence. *Aggression & Violent Behavior* (10): 1-30. 2004.

Chapter 5 - Advanced Psychological Processes and Treatments - questions

1. Which one of the following is a characteristic of temperament?

A. Inequity
B. Distractibility
C. Control
D. Wickedness
E. Shabbiness

2. Which one of the following characteristics is present in an infant with a difficult temperament?

A. Playful
B. Irregular sleeping pattern
C. Regular eating pattern
D. Withdrawal from new situations in a mild manner
E. Relatively inactive

3. Which one of the following statements is true with regards to the stability of temperamental characteristics over time?

A. It is high in early infant years
B. Tendency to approach and avoid unfamiliar events is highly stable
C. Toddlers' temperament predicts their emotional and behavioural characteristics for later in life
D. It entirely depends on environmental factors
E. It entirely depends on genetic factors

4. Which one of the following statements is true with regards to development of personality?

A. Child temperament and adult personality traits share few features in common
B. Individual differences in youths' personalities can be described in terms of Big Five personality traits observed in adults
C. Personality changes are relatively uncommon in adult years
D. Personality is only slightly stable in preschool years
E. Personality is moderately stable in preschool years

5. Which one of the following statements is true for longitudinal course and outcome of personality disorders?

A. Personality psychopathology improves very slowly over time
B. Personality psychopathology is stable over time
C. Maladaptive personality traits are more stable than personality disorder diagnoses
D. Personality psychopathology eventually completely recovers
E. There is no difference in the stability of maladaptive personality traits and personality disorder diagnoses

6. Which one of the following factors is related to development and maintenance of anxiety disorders in children?

A. Excessive parental control
B. Little supervision
C. More than two siblings
D. Time spent in day care
E. Both parents in full-time work

7. Which one of the following statements is true for the effects of day care on children's well being and attachments?

A. Children who spend more than 20 hours per week in day care are more aggressive
B. Children who spend more than 20 hours per week in day care are less compliant
C. Children who spend more than 20 hours per week in day care are insecurely attached to their mothers
D. Cognitive development is usually affected either positively or not at all
E. Day care centres with low ratio of staff to children have positive effect on children's development

8. Which one of the following syndromes is not described by John Bowlby as a consequence of maternal deprivation during a 'critical period'?

A. Affectionless psychopathy
B. Intellectual retardation
C. Conduct disorders
D. Acute distress syndrome

E. Capgras syndrome

9. Which one of the following statements is true with regards to the effects of parental divorce on the child's mental health?

A. Antisocial behaviour may reduce
B. Anxiety levels are likely to reduce
C. Parental bereavement in comparison to parental divorce has more mental health consequences for a child
D. Antisocial behaviour increases after a divorce in a highly dysfunctional family
E. Child's temperament has no bearing on the outcome

10. Which one of the following statements is true with regards to environmental influences on language development in children?
A. Larger family size is associated with faster speech development
B. Being middle class is associated with delayed language development
C. There is little difference in males and females
D. Children in bilingual homes have slow language development
E. Prolonged first stage of labour is associated with slow language development

11. Which one of the following statements is true with regards to the effects of various parenting behaviours?

A. Disorganised style produces secure attachment
B. Abusive parenting is a strong predictor of later psychopathology
C. Sensitive responsive style results in contradictory behaviours
D. Parental warmth is negatively associated with child's self esteem
E. Parenting style is the major cause of an infant's attachment behaviours

12. Which one of the following mental illnesses is more likely to be diagnosed in upper social classes?

A. Schizophrenia
B. Alcohol dependence
C. Bipolar affective disorder
D. Organic psychosis
E. Depressive episodes in women

13. Which one of the following statements is true for memory?

A. During encoding of memory right hemisphere is more active
B. During retrieval of memory left hemisphere is more active
C. Working memory lasts for minutes
D. Sensory memory lasts for few hundreds of milliseconds
E. Explicit memory is unconscious

14. Which one of the following statements is true for transient global amnesia?

A. Occurs in young age
B. Common in females
C. Transient dysfunction in limbic-hippocampal circuits is implicated
D. Characterised by mutism
E. Loss of personal identity

15. Which one of the following statements is true for psychogenic amnesia?

A. Loss of personal identity
B. Fugue states usually last for weeks
C. No resemblance to organic amnesia
D. It is rarely associated with depressed mood
E. It is sometimes referred to as functional anterograde amnesia

16. Which one of the following statements is true for neuropsychological sequelae of PTSD?

A. It is associated with semantic memory loss
B. It is associated with procedural memory loss
C. Executive functions are spared in PTSD
D. Memory loss is only related to the traumatic event
E. PTSD and memory impairment are strongly connected

17. Which one of the following statements is true for neuropsychological sequelae of depression?

A. It is associated with procedural memory loss
B. Memory loss can be associated with functional and structural changes in hippocampus

C. It is associated with semantic memory loss
D. No structural change in prefrontal cortex
E. Decision making and planning is preserved

18. Which one of the following statements is true for anterograde amnesia?

A. Failure to encode semantic information is the fundamental memory deficit
B. Hippocampal damage produces deficits in recognition memory only
C. Perirhinal pathology produces deficits in recall memory only
D. Memories based on recollection are severely impaired
E. Memories based on familiarity judgements is spared

19. Which one of the following statements is true for patients with medial temporal amnesia when compared to patients with frontal lobe amnesia?

A. They show slow forgetting on recall tasks
B. Less likely to respond to provision of specific category cues
C. Have less fundamental amnesic deficit
D. Functional imaging shows little difference
E. Have more executive deficit

20. Which one of the following is true for a patient with damage to Wernicke's area?

A. Abnormal speech
B. Preserved comprehension
C. Conduction dysphasia
D. Dysfluent expressive dysphasia
E. Fluent receptive dysphasia

21. Which one of the following statements is true with regards to a person's memory capacity?

A. Maximum of ten items can be stored in immediate memory
B. Phonics can be used to enhance long-term memory
C. Memory cannot be improved
D. Chunking is used to enhance retention in immediate memory
E. Mnemonics enhance immediate memory by increasing the number of chunks

22. Which one of the following statements is true for CAMCOG?

A. It incorporates CAMDEX
B. CAMDEX incorporates CAMCOG
C. It is a test for praxis only
D. It is an intelligence test
E. It is a measure of premorbid IQ

23. Which one of the following is true for the clock drawing test?

A. It provides qualitative information only
B. It is an integral part of MMSE
C. It is a memory test
D. It meets defined criteria for a cognitive screening instrument
E. In combination with short performance test it is a highly specific test for dementia

24. Which one of the following is not a verbal subtest of Wechsler's Adult Intelligence scale?

A. Matrix reasoning
B. Information
C. Comprehension
D. Arithmetic
E. Digit span

25. Which one of the following statements is true with regards to International Personality Disorder Examination (IPDE)?

A. It is a structured clinical interview
B. It is compatible with ICD-10
C. It is not compatible with DSM-IV
D. It is immune to feigning
E. It considers a behaviour to be a personality trait only if it is present for 2 years

26. Which one of the following tests is not an objective personality test?

A. Minnesota Multiphasic Personality Inventory (MMPI)
B. California Psychological Inventory (CPI)
C. Eysenck Personality Questionnaire (EPQ)
D. Thematic Appreciation Test (TAT)

E. Hostility and Direction of Hostility Questionnaire (HDHQ)

27. Which one of the following is not a factor of the 5-factor theory of personality?

A. Openness to experience
B. Neuroticism
C. Introversion
D. Agreeableness
E. Conscientiousness

28. Which one of the following statements is true for affect dysregulation with cluster A personality disorders?

A. Consistent under regulation of the affects of fear and terror
B. Under regulation of positive affects
C. Under regulation of all affects in schizoid personality disorder
D. Positive affects usually experienced only when with others
E. Over regulation of feelings of empathy

29. Which one of the following statements is true for effects of CBT on brain functioning in anxiety disorders?

A. It does not produce any biological change
B. It can increase level of activity of rostral caudate nucleus in OCD
C. It has no effect on frontal metabolism
D. It can normalise occipital metabolism in spider phobia
E. It can normalise frontal metabolism in social phobia

30. Which one of the following statements is true with regards to psychotherapy in personality disorders?

A. In DBT patient may contact therapist by phone between sessions
B. CAT is appropriate for schizotypal personality disorder
C. Psychodynamic therapy is of proven benefit in patients with personality disorder
D. Schema focused CBT disregards early maladaptive schemas and concentrates on new schemas
E. IPT has a proven role in antisocial personality disorder

31. Which one of the following statements is true for cognitive analytic therapy?

A. It is an open-ended therapy
B. Reciprocal role formation is a key feature
C. It is based on Pavlovian therapy
D. Reformulation is done by the patient
E. Reformulation is based on here and now principle

32. Which one of the following is true with regards to the treatment goal in stage 1 of treatment in Dialectical Behaviour therapy?

A. Resolve a sense of incompleteness
B. Replace 'quiet desperation' with non-traumatic emotional experience
C. Achieve 'ordinary' happiness
D. Achieve behavioural control
E. Reduce ongoing disorders and problems in living

33. Which one of the following is true for interpersonal psychotherapy?

A. Therapy is carried out in four phases
B. There are possible five focal areas in which therapy can be focused
C. Patient is given a sick role
D. It has proven to be useful in anorexia nervosa
E. It has an intrapsychic element as well

34. Which one of the following is not a domain of schemas used in schema-focused cognitive therapy?

A. Disconnection and rejection
B. Impaired autonomy and performance
C. Impaired limits
D. Self-directness
E. Over-vigilance and inhibition

35. Which one of the following statements is true with regards to progression of personality disorders?

A. Cluster A patients generally improve with age
B. Cluster B patients generally remain unchanged with age
C. Cluster C patients generally worsen with age
D. 20% of schizotypal personality disorder patients develop schizophrenia
E. When patients with obsessional personality disorder worsen with age they are more likely to develop depression than OCD

Chapter 6 - Advanced Psychological Processes and Treatments - answers

1. **B** - The term temperament is used to refer to mood-related personality characteristics. There are nine characteristics of temperament identified by Thomas and Chess in the New York Longitudinal Study, namely, distractibility, activity, regularity (rhythmicity), intensity of reaction, quality of mood, persistence and attention span, initial reaction (approach or withdrawal) and sensitivity (sensory threshold of responsiveness to stimuli). These nine characteristics were combined to define three broad temperament types in infants. About 40% have 'easy temperament', 10% have 'difficult temperament' and 15% have 'slow to warm up temperament'. The remaining 35% of the infants are not rated high or low on any of the defining dimensions.

    Smith, *et al.*: 'Psychological Development'. In Atkinson & Hilgard's *Introduction to Psychology*. 14th ed. Graphic World Publishing Services, Thomson Wadsworth. 2003.

2. **B** - Infants who are irritable, have irregular sleeping and eating patterns, and respond intensely and negatively to new situations are classified as having a 'difficult temperament'. Infants who are playful, are regular in their sleeping and eating patterns, and adapt readily to new situations are classified as having an 'easy temperament'. Infants who are relatively inactive, tend to withdraw from new situations in a mild way, and require more time than easy infants to adapt to new situations are classified as having a 'slow to warm up temperament'.

    Smith, *et al.*: 'Psychological Development'. In Atkinson & Hilgard's *Introduction to Psychology*. 14th ed. Graphic World Publishing Services, Thomson Wadsworth. 2003.

3. **C** - Research has shown that the stability of temperamental characteristics in the early infant years is low. However, temperament of a toddler has a predictive value for his emotional and behavioural characteristics later in life. Research has also revealed that the tendency to approach or avoid new events, a characteristic of temperament, remains moderately stable over time. There is also evidence, based on identical and fraternal twin studies, that both genetic and environmental factors have a role to play in shaping infants' temperament over time.

Smith, *et al.*: 'Psychological Development'. In Atkinson & Hilgard's *Introduction to Psychology*. 14th ed. Graphic World Publishing Services, Thomson Wadsworth. 2003.

4. **E** – Recent work on normal personality development in children and adolescents points to several conclusions that are relevant for understanding personality pathology. First, child temperament and adult personality traits share many features in common. Second, youths' individual differences can be described in terms of the Big Five personality traits observed in adults. Third, personality is already moderately stable by the preschool years, but considerable personality change occurs well into the adult years.

    Shiner, R L: A developmental perspective on personality disorders: lessons from research on normal personality development in childhood and adolescence. *J Personal Disord* 19(2): 202-210. 2005.

5. **C** – The notion of personality disorders (PDs) as stable disorders has persisted despite traditional follow-up studies showing that fewer than 50% of patients diagnosed with PDs retained these diagnoses over time. Because these studies had methodological limitations, more rigorous large-scale studies of the naturalistic course of PDs have been conducted. The results indicate (1) personality psychopathology improves over time at unexpectedly significant rates; (2) maladaptive personality traits are more stable than PD diagnoses; (3) although personality psychopathology improves, residual effects can be seen in the form of persistent functional impairment, continuing behavioural problems, reduced future quality of life, and ongoing Axis I psychopathology; (4) improvement in personality psychopathology may eventually be associated with reduction in ongoing personal and social burden.

    Skodol, A E: Longitudinal course and outcome of personality disorders. *Psychiatr Clin North Am* 31(3): 495-503, viii. 2008.

6. **A** – Parenting styles of anxious children have been described as overprotecting, ambivalent, rejecting, and hostile. Retrospective reports of adults with anxiety disorders show that these adults

view their parents as over-controlling and less affectionate. Studies of families of children with anxiety indicate that these families score lower on indices of child independence and participation in recreational activities, and higher on indices of hostility/ conflict than families of non-anxious children. Literature review of the parenting and child-rearing practices research suggests that excessive parental control is related to the development and maintenance of anxiety disorders in children. Moreover, having an anxious family member (e.g. parent) also has been shown to increase risk of distress and dysfunction in family relationships. Based on the influence of family-related factors in children with anxiety disorders, psychological interventions should therefore have a family-focused component to it as well.

Mcleod, *et al.*: Examining the association between parenting and childhood anxiety: A meta-analysis. *Clinical Psychology Review* 27(2), 155-172. 2007.

7. D – Although parenting is a stronger and more consistent predictor of children's development than early child-care experience, higher quality day care predicts higher vocabulary scores. Any negative effects tend to be emotional and positive effects tend to be social; however, this is only true for a reasonable to a good quality day care. Poor quality care can have negative effects on children, regardless of their home environment.

    Belsky, J, *et al.*: Are There Long-Term Effects of Early Child Care? *Child Development* 78(2), 681-701. 2007.

8. E – Bowlby described a 'critical period' for maternal deprivation between the age of 6 months and 3 years. He described consequences of prolonged maternal deprivation during the critical period as developmental language delay, indiscriminate affection seeking, shallow relationships, enuresis, aggression, lack of empathy, social disinhibition, dwarfism, attention seeking and over- activity in school. These symptoms can broadly be distinguished as four syndromes, namely, acute distress syndrome, conduct disorders,

intellectual retardation and affectionless psychopathy. Rutter has done extensive work in this area since.

Rutter, M, *et al*.: *Research and Innovation on the Road to Modern Child Psychiatry*. RCPsych Publications. 2001.

9. **A** – A process-oriented approach to parental divorce locates the experience within the social and developmental context of children's lives, providing greater insight into how parental divorce produces vulnerability in some children and resiliency in others. Studies have shown that, even before marital break-up, children whose parents later divorce exhibit higher levels of anxiety or depression and antisocial behaviour than children whose parents remain married. There is a further increase in child anxiety or depression but not antisocial behaviour associated with the event of parental divorce itself. Controlling for pre-divorce parental socioeconomic and psychosocial resources fully accounts for poorer child mental health among children whose parents later divorce, but does not explain the divorce-specific increase in anxiety or depression. Finally, a significant interaction between parental divorce and pre-divorce levels of family dysfunction suggests that children's antisocial behaviour decreases when marriages in highly dysfunctional families are dissolved.

Strohschein, L: Parental Divorce and Child Mental Health Trajectories. *Journal of Marriage and Family* 67(5), 1286-1300. 2005.

10. **C** – Larger family size, intrauterine growth retardation, prolonged second stage of labour and being a twin are associated with slow language development. Being a middle class is associated with faster language development, whereas living in bilingual homes is not a disadvantage. Genetic and environmental influences on language ability and disability are quantitatively and qualitatively similar for males and females.

Kovas, Y, et al.: Genetic Influences in Different Aspects of Language Development: The Etiology of Language Skills in 4.5-Year-Old Twins. *Child Development* 76(3), 632-651. 2005.

11. **B** – Baumrind described four types of parenting styles: authoritative, authoritarian, permissive and neglectful. Authoritative style is characterised by high expectations of compliance to parental rules and directions, an open dialogue about those rules and behaviours, and a child-centred approach. This style generally leads children to become more independent, confident and successful in their life. Authoritarian parenting style is characterised by high expectations of conformity and compliance to parental rules and directions. Much is expected of their child by authoritarian parents, but they do not explain or discuss the rules at all. Authoritarian parents tend to punish their children more, resulting in higher rates of later psychopathology in them. Permissive parenting is characterised as having few behavioural expectations for the child and is characterised by warm affect. Parents are nurturing and accepting, but non-demanding. Neglectful parenting, also known as nonconformist parenting, is similar to permissive parenting, but the parent does not care much about the child. The parents are generally not involved in their child's life, but will provide basic needs.

In general, sensitive responsiveness by parents produces secure attachment. Moreover, parental warmth and support buffers children against externalising and antisocial behaviour and increases the child's self-esteem. Although parenting styles play a significant role in attachment behaviours, they are not the only cause of shaping an infant's attachment behaviours as the infant's own inborn temperament has a huge role to play as well.

Baumrind, D: Parental disciplinary patterns and social competence in children. *Youth and Society* 9, 238-276. 1978.

12. **C** – Schizophrenia, organic psychosis, depression in females, personality disorders, parasuicide and alcohol dependence are

more likely to be diagnosed in lower socioeconomic classes, whereas bipolar affective disorder and eating disorders are more likely to be diagnosed in higher socioeconomic classes. Downward social drift in schizophrenia and the role of environmental stresses are possible explanations for a relationship between social classes and mental illnesses. However, the social adversity in childhood and foetal life is independently associated with the risk of developing schizophrenia and other psychoses later in life.

Wicks, *et al.*: Social Adversity in Childhood and the Risk of Developing Psychosis: A National Cohort Study. *Am J Psychiatry* 162: 1652-1657, 2005.

13. **D** – There are three stages of memory which include encoding, storage and retrieval. Research has revealed that most of the brain regions activated during encoding are in the left hemisphere and the most regions activated during retrieval are in the right hemisphere. There are three kinds of memory which differ in terms of their temporal characteristics: sensory memory lasts over a few hundreds of milliseconds; working memory lasts for seconds; and long-term memory operates over time ranging from minutes to years. Different memories for different kinds of information are stored differently: explicit memory is one in which a person consciously recalls an event as occurring in a specific time and place; implicit memory is one in which a person unconsciously remembers information of various sorts; for example, information required to drive a car.

Smith, *et al.*: 'Psychological Development'. In Atkinson & Hilgard's *Introduction to Psychology.* 14th ed. Graphic World Publishing Services, Thomson Wadsworth. 2003.

14. **C** – Transient global amnesia is a temporary version of amnesic syndrome, occurring in the middle aged or elderly, more commonly in men. It is thought to be due to transient dysfunction in limbic-hippocampal circuits lasting for several hours to 24 hours. It is characterised by repetitive questioning and often confusion,

but without loss of personal identity. It can be accompanied by headache, nausea or photophobia and can be preceded by physical or emotional stressors.

Schott, J M, *et al.*: Ischemic Bilateral Hippocampal Dysfunction During Transient Global Amnesia. *Neurology* 70(20), 1940-41. 2008.

15. **A** – Psychological forms of memory loss can either be 'global' or 'situation-specific'. The former refers to a profound loss of past memories, often encompassing the sense of personal identity, and the latter to memory loss for a particular incident or part of an incident.

Global amnesia is exemplified by the so-called 'fugue state', sometimes known as 'functional retrograde amnesia'. The fugue state refers, in essence, to a syndrome consisting of a sudden loss of all autobiographical memories and knowledge of self or personal identity, usually associated with a period of wandering, for which there is a subsequent amnesic gap upon recovery. Fugue states usually last a few hours or days only: if prolonged, the suspicion of simulation must always arise. There appear to be three main predisposing factors for fugue episodes. First, fugue states are always preceded by a severe, precipitating stress, such as marital or emotional discord, bereavement, financial problems, a charge of offending or stress during wartime. Secondly, depressed mood is an extremely common antecedent for psychogenic fugue states. Whether the individual in the fugue is psychotic, neurotic, or psychopathic, depression seems to start off the fugue. The third factor is a history of a transient, organic amnesia from such causes as epilepsy, head injury or alcoholic blackouts. It appears that patients who have previously experienced a transient organic amnesia, and then become depressed and/or suicidal, are particularly likely to go into a fugue in the face of a severe precipitating stress. The clinical and neuropsychological phenomena in such cases bear interesting resemblances to organic amnesia.

Situation-specific amnesia can arise in a variety of circumstances, including committing an offence, being the victim of an offence or of child sexual abuse, and in a variety of other circumstances resulting in post-traumatic stress disorder.

Kopelman, M D: Disorders of memory. *Brain* 125: 2152-2190. 2002.

16. **E** – PTSD and memory impairment are strongly connected, and PTSD appears to particularly affect executive functions and episodic memory. There has, however, been a suggestion in literature that exposure to a traumatic event can lead to executive problems, regardless of a diagnosis of chronic PTSD. Structural and functional imaging techniques have identified abnormalities in the brains of people with PTSD in regions known to be important for memory functioning. Nevertheless, studies investigating cognitive functioning in people with PTSD have reported widely varying results. There is reasonable evidence of frontal lobe involvement; memory deficits caused by hippocampal involvement have been more difficult to detect.

Isaac, C L, *et al.*: Is posttraumatic stress disorder associated with specific deficits in episodic memory? *Clin Psychol Rev* 26: 939-955. 2006.

17. **B** – The typical cognitive symptoms of depression include poor decision making and planning, memory and concentration problems, inattention, irritability, interpersonal difficulties and general slowing down. Association between episodic memory deficits and depression has been identified which may be associated with functional and structural changes, particularly in the hippocampus and prefrontal cortex.

Frodl, T S, *et al.*: Depression-Related Variation in Brain Morphology Over 3 Years, Effects of Stress? *Arch Gen Psychiatry* 65(10): 1156-1165. 2008.

18. **D** – It has been hypothesised that hippocampal damage produces a deficit only in recall memory, whereas perirhinal pathology implicates recognition memory as well. The evidence suggests that memories based on 'recollection' (and its subjective counterpart, 'remembering') are severely impaired in amnesia, and that those based on familiarity judgements (or 'knowing') are also significantly impaired, although less severely so. The hypothesis that a failure to encode semantic information is the fundamental

memory deficit in amnesia is not supported. The conventional wisdom is that priming is spared in amnesia, and that damage to sites of pathology beyond the medial temporal lobes is required to produce impaired priming (e.g. involving occipital circuitry). However, amnesic patients do show impaired priming in certain experimental conditions, e.g. in 'difficult' tasks where baseline responding has been controlled or in associative learning. This implicates a contribution of medial temporal/diencephalic structures in priming in these circumstances.

Kopelman, M D: Disorders of memory. *Brain* 125: 2152-2190. 2002.

19. B – Lesion and neuroimaging studies indicate a closer interaction and overlap in function than was previously assumed between the frontal lobe and medial temporal structures engaged in memory formation. Whilst a broad distinction between executive processes and encoding/retrieval mechanisms remains valid, there is considerable overlap in the effect of focal lesions involving these brain regions, and in the brain activations associated with specific memory tasks. However, lesion studies indicate that medial temporal patients show faster forgetting on recall tasks than frontal patients, and are less likely to respond to the provision of specific category cues, suggesting a more fundamental amnesic deficit. Similarly, some functional imaging studies suggest that medial temporal activations are more closely related to successful or incremental remembering than are frontal activations. Lesion studies indicate that there may be differences between specific sites of frontal pathology on temporal context memory and in effects upon recall and recognition memory.

Kopelman, M D: Disorders of memory. *Brain* 125: 2152-2190. 2002.

20. E – Damage to Wernicke's area disrupts comprehension of both written and spoken language. Speech is normal in rhythm and tone, as Broca's area is intact, but the content is abnormal. Patient

is unaware that his dysphasic speech is difficult for others to understand. He tends to use meaningless words and paraphrasias. Therefore, dysphasia resulting from damage to Wernicke's area is a fluent receptive dysphasia.

Dysfluent expressive dysphasia results from damage to Broca's area. This results in slow hesitant speech lacking connecting words. Speech sounds agrammatical, of which the person is fully aware as his comprehension is normal due to Wernicke's area being intact.

Conduction dysphasia results from damage to the arcuate fasciculus; as a result, a person cannot repeat what he hears. The patient can understand what is said because Wernicke's area is intact and can produce fluent speech because Broca's area is intact, but cannot transmit what was understood to the speech centre because the connecting links between the areas are damaged.

Smith, *et al.*: 'Psychological Development'. In Atkinson & Hilgard's *Introduction to Psychology*. 14th ed. Graphic World Publishing Services, Thomson Wadsworth. 2003.

21. **D** – Up to 7 ± 2 items can be stored in immediate/working memory. Several pieces of information can be associated together to form a single item to enhance the amount of retention in immediate memory. However, the capacity of immediate memory cannot be increased beyond 7 ± 2 chunks. Mnemonic systems use imagery while encoding to aid memory; pieces of information are associated together with one another according to various mental pictorial schemes or other cognitive techniques. Imagery is also used in the key word method, which is very helpful in learning the vocabulary of a foreign language.

Smith, *et al.*: 'Psychological Development'. In Atkinson & Hilgard's *Introduction to Psychology*. 14th ed. Graphic World Publishing Services, Thomson Wadsworth. 2003.

22. **B** – The CAMCOG, which forms part of the CAMDEX interview, is a brief neuropsychological battery designed to assess the range of cognitive functions required for a diagnosis of dementia, and to detect mild degrees of cognitive impairment. In contrast to the Mini-Mental State Examination, total CAMCOG scores are well distributed and there is no ceiling effect. Examination of the association between CAMCOG scores and socio-demographic variables (age, sex, education and social class) shows that each exerts a significant, and independent, effect upon performance. CAMCOG also includes a number of subscales which assess individual areas of cognitive function. Of the eight major subscales (orientation, language, memory, attention, praxis, calculation, abstract thinking, perception), age is significantly related to all but attention; sex with attention, praxis, calculation and perception; education with language and abstract thinking; and social class with language and perception. In general, the combination of brevity and breadth of the CAMCOG, along with its distributional properties, makes it an attractive neuropsychological test.

Huppert, F A, *et al.*: CAMCOG—a concise neuropsychological test to assist dementia diagnosis: socio-demographic determinants in an elderly population sample. *Br J Clin Psychol* 34 (Pt 4): 529-541. 1995.

23. **D** – The clock drawing test meets defined criteria for a cognitive screening instrument. It taps into a wide range of cognitive abilities, including executive functions, and is quick and easy to administer and score, with excellent acceptability by subjects. The clock drawing test in combination with the MMSE or short performance test is an easily administered, non-threatening and highly sensitive screening test for dementia in the setting of a memory clinic.

Schramm, U, *et al.*: Psychometric properties of Clock Drawing Test and MMSE or Short Performance Test in dementia screening in a memory clinic population. *Int J Geriatr Psychiatry* 17(3): 254-260. 2002.

24. **A** – Wechsler's Adult Intelligence scale is a general test of intelligence. It quantifies IQ as an index score. The median full-scale IQ is centred at 100, with a standard deviation of 15. The scale consists of six verbal and five performance/nonverbal subtests. The verbal subtests include information, comprehension, arithmetic, similarities, vocabulary and digit span. In addition, the verbal subtests include one optional subtest called letter-number sequencing. The performance subtests include picture completion, block design, picture arrangement, symbol search and object assembly. In addition, performance subtests also include two optional subtests called digit symbol coding and matrix reasoning.

Kaplan & Saccuzzo: *Psychological testing: Principles, applications and issues.* Thomson Wadsworth. 2005.

25. **B** – The IPDE is a semi-structured clinical interview compatible with the ICD-10 and DSM-IV. It has been translated into various languages, including Dutch, French, German, Hindi, Japanese, Kannada, Norwegian, Swahili, Tamil, Danish, Estonian, Greek, Italian, Russian and Spanish. The IPDE considers a behaviour to be a personality trait only if it exists for at least a span of five years. The IPDE also requires that behaviour indicative of at least one criterion of a personality disorder be present prior to age 25, before that particular disorder can be diagnosed. The remaining criteria for the disorder may become evident after age 25, provided the requirement of five years' duration is met. This rule exists for each individual disorder. However, when a subject meets all the requirements for a diagnosis except that regarding onset by age 25, an optional diagnosis may be recorded with the designation, late onset.

There are some limitations of the IPDE as it is essentially a self-report instrument, and assumes that subjects are capable of providing valid descriptions of disturbances in their personality. Some patients may exaggerate, whereas others may under-report disturbances in their behaviour, hence leaving the IPDE potentially vulnerable to feigning.

Loranger, A W: *International Personality Disorder Examination – IPDE Manual.* American Psychiatric Press. 1995.

26. **D** – Thematic Appreciation Test is a commonly used projective personality test. Other common projective personality tests include Rorschach (inkblot test) and Sentence Completion Test (SCT). Projective tests have a potentially unlimited number of possible responses to items or stimuli, hence considerable time and training is required for scoring.
On the other hand, objective tests have a limited set of responses, facilitating reliability and ease of scoring. The MMPI consists of 550 statements about attitudes, psychological symptoms, physical systems, previous experiences and emotional reactions. The CPI measures up to 18 traits which are usually part of normal personality. The EPQ has 90 items rating the person on the basis of extraversion, introversion and neuroticism. The HDHQ is used to measure relationships.

Smith, *et al.*: 'Psychological Development'. In Atkinson & Hilgard's *Introduction to Psychology.* 14th ed. Graphic World Publishing Services, Thomson Wadsworth. 2003.

27. **C** – The factors of 5-factor theory of personality include extraversion, neuroticism, conscientiousness, agreeableness and openness to experience. A number of meta-analysis have confirmed the predictive value of the 5-factor theory across a wide range of behaviours. These factors have also been replicated across many cultures.

Saulsman & Page: The five factor model and personality disorder empirical literature: A meta analytic review. *Clinical Psychology Review* 23, 1055-1085. 2004.

28. A – Individuals who have experienced insecure attachment are at risk of developing dysregulated and disorganised affective systems. There is evidence that childhood adversity is a risk factor for developing personality disorder.

Affective dysregulations associated with Cluster A personality disorders include consistent under-regulation of the affects of fear and terror, over-regulation of positive affects with a narrow range of affective expression. There is over-regulation of all affects in schizoid personality disorder.

Affective dysregulations associated with Cluster B personality disorders include dysregulation (under or over) of both positive and negative affects, but predominantly demonstrated with fear, anger, sadness and anxiety. There is under-regulation of fear, arousal and anger, and over-regulation of feelings of empathy, remorse and guilt in antisocial and narcissistic personality disorders. Under-regulation of most affects is seen in histrionic personality disorder.

Affective dysregulations associated with Cluster C personality disorders include under-regulation of social emotions, e.g. shame and guilt, and under-regulation of anxiety and sadness. Positive affects are usually experienced only when with others.

Sarkar & Adshead: Personality disorders as disorganisation of attachment and affect regulation. *Advances in Psychiatric Treatment* 12: 297-305. 2006.

29. E – There is evidence to suggest that CBT and drug treatment can result in similar changes in brain functioning in anxiety patients. CBT and imipramine both show reductions in over-activation of rostral caudate nucleus in obsessive compulsive disorder patients. CBT and citalopram both normalise frontal metabolism in social phobia. Also in spider phobia, CBT normalises the frontal metabolism. In depression, CBT affects medial prefrontal cortex, anterior cingulate cortex and hippocampus, while pharmacotherapy affects limbic subcortical areas. These findings suggest that a psychotherapeutic approach, such as CBT, has the potential to modify the dysfunctional neural circuitry associated with anxiety disorders and depression.

Goldapple, K, *et al.*: Modulation of cortical-limbic pathways in major depression: treatment-specific effects of cognitive behavior therapy. *Arch Gen Psychiatry* 61: 34-41. 2004.

30. A – Some patients with borderline personality disorder benefit from CAT and DBT. Psychodynamic therapy has no proven benefit in personality disorder; however, some modified approaches are being used for borderline and narcissistic personality disorders. There is a view that in severe personality disorder psychodynamic psychotherapy should be contraindicated. In schema-focused CBT early maladaptive schemas and behaviours are identified and modified.

Davison & Tyrer: 'Psychosocial treatment in personality disorder'. In *Personality Disorders: diagnosis, management and cause*. Ed. Tyrer, P. Oxford: Butterworth Heinemann. 2000.

31. B – The key features of CAT include: (a) focus on 'reciprocal role procedures', which are formed through the internalisation of socially meaningful, inter-subjective experience and subsequently determine both interpersonal behaviours and self-management; and (b) the practical emphasis on the joint creation of descriptions of these, which serve to enlarge patients' capacity for self-reflection and change and therapists' ability to provide reparative, non-collusive relationships. Typically, the therapy comprises of 16 sessions. In the first 4-6 sessions the therapist collects all the relevant information. After that, as mentioned above, reformulation is done jointly and the therapist writes the reformulation letter to the patient. Particular attention is given to understanding the connection between childhood patterns of behaviour and their impact on adult life. At the end, both therapist and the patient write goodbye letters reflecting on the therapy.

Ryle, A, & Kerr, I B: *Introducing Cognitive Analytic Therapy: Principles and Practice*. Chichester: John Wiley & Sons. 2002.

32. D – DBT is conceptualised to be occurring in four stages. Primary

focus in stage 1 is to achieve stabilisation and behavioural control. Behavioural targets in this stage include decreasing life-threatening suicidal behaviours, decreasing therapy interfering behaviours, decreasing quality of life-interfering behaviours and increasing behavioural skills. The treatment goal for stage 2 is to replace 'quiet desperation' with non-traumatic emotional experience; stage 3 is to achieve 'ordinary' happiness and unhappiness and reduce ongoing disorders and problems in living; and stage 4 is to resolve a sense of incompleteness and achieve joy.

Dimeff & Linehan: Dialectical behavior therapy in a nutshell. *The California Psychologist* 34: 10-13. 2001.

33. **C** – IPT is an effective treatment developed for major depression and has also shown benefit in other conditions, including bulimia nervosa, dysthymia, depression in adolescent and elderly and borderline personality disorder. It is a brief-focused therapy that concentrates on the patients' current interpersonal relationships. It is usually on a weekly basis lasting for sixteen sessions divided into three parts: a beginning, middle and an end. In the initial sessions the diagnosis is made and the patient is educated about the condition and given a sick role. This allows the patient to mark a change and make some space to work on getting better. One of the four focal areas – complicated bereavement, role transitions, interpersonal role disputes and interpersonal sensitivity – is identified for the focus of the remaining therapy. The last few sessions are focused on ending.

Markowitz, J: Evidence-Based Psychotherapies for Depression. *Journal of Occupational & Environmental Med* 50(4): 437-440. 2008.

34. **D** – Schema-focused cognitive therapy is used in treating personality disorders. It is based on addressing early maladaptive schemas. There are five domains of schemas. Schemas in the domain of 'disconnection and rejection' result from early

experiences of a detached, explosive, unpredictable, or abusive family environment. People with these schemas expect that their needs for security, safety, stability, nurturance, and empathy in intimate or family relationships will not be met in a consistent or predictable way. Schemas in the 'impaired autonomy and performance' domain have to do with expectations about oneself and the environment that interfere with one's ability to separate and function independently and one's perceived ability to survive alone. The typical family of origin is enmeshed, undermining of the child's judgement, or overprotective. Schemas in the 'impaired limits' domain relate to deficiencies in internal limits, respect and responsibility to others, or meeting realistic personal goals. The typical family origin is permissiveness and indulgence. Schemas in the 'other-directness' domain relate to an excessive focus on meeting the needs of others, at the expense of one's own needs. The typical family origin is based on conditional acceptance, whereby children suppress normal needs and emotions in order to gain attention, approval and love. Schemas in the 'over-vigilance and inhibition' domain involve an excessive focus of controlling, suppressing, or ignoring of one's emotions and spontaneous feelings in order to avoid making mistakes, or meeting rigged internalised rules. Typical family origins are domination and suppression of feelings, or a bleak environment where performance standards and self-control take priority over pleasure and playfulness

Young, J E, *et al.*: *Schema Therapy: A Practitioner's Guide*. Guildford Press. 2003.

35. **E** – Cluster A patients generally worsen, Cluster B improve and Cluster C stay the same with age. 50% of schizotypal personality disorder patients develop schizophrenia over time.

Tyrer & Seivewright: 'Outcome of personality disorder'. In *Personality Disorders: diagnosis, management and cause*. Ed. Tyrer, P. Oxford: Butterworth Heinemann. 2000.

Chapter 7 - Genetics - questions

1. A pregnant lady tells you that her husband's twin brother suffers from Schizophrenia. She wants to know the chances of her child developing schizophrenia. Is it:

A. 5-10%
B. 12-15%
C. 12-20%
D. 20-25%
E. 22-30%

2. Which one of the following statements about the MECP2 gene is true?

A. Mutations in the MECP2 gene almost exclusively cause disorder in females
B. A genetic disorder is seen in males when the MECP2 gene on the Y chromosome is affected
C. MECP2 gene mutation is not seen in males
D. MECP2 gene mutation is known to be found on both X and Y chromosomes
E. Genetic disorder caused by mutation on MECP2 gene is inherited in 30% of the cases

3. Mutations in the alpha-synuclein gene are known to cause:

A. Wilson's disease
B. Parkinson's disease
C. Huntington's disease
D. Williams disease
E. Down syndrome

4. A 28-year-old female suffering from bipolar affective disorder wants to have a child. She wants to know: what is the chance of her child having a psychiatric disorder?

A. 25%
B. 33%
C. 40%
D. 50%
E. 65%

5. Which of the following genes implicated in the aetiology of
    schizophrenia has been found to play a significant part in
    regulating integration of newly generated neurons in the adult
    brain?

A. DISC1
B. DISC3
C. DAOA
D. DTNBP1
E. DAOB

6. A 38-year-old male is referred to you for anxiety. Apart from
    anxiety, he complains of tics and involuntary movements. He also
    feels that his memory is getting worse. He tells you that his father
    also suffered from similar symptoms before dying at the age of 52.
    You notice that at times he grimaces inappropriately. The disease
    he is suffering from is most likely to be due to a genetic defect on
    which of the following chromosomes?

A. Chromosome 2
B. Chromosome 3
C. Chromosome 4
D. Chromosome 5
E. Chromosome 6

7. Recent research has shown mutations in Progranulin to be
    associated with which of the following disorders?

A. Huntington's disease
B. Schizophrenia
C. Frontotemporal dementia
D. Bipolar affective disorder
E. Lewy body dementia

8. Data from separate twin samples with bipolar disorder versus
    unipolar depression probands suggests that:

A. 25% of the genetic liability to mania is independent of the liability
    to depression
B. 36% of the genetic liability to mania is independent of the liability
    to depression
C. 71% of the genetic liability to mania is independent of the liability
    to depression

D. 27% of the genetic liability to depression is independent of the liability to mania

E. 50% of the genetic liability to depression is independent of the liability to mania

9. Several putative susceptibility genes for schizophrenia have been identified; however, the causative allele or the mechanism by which they predispose to schizophrenia is still unclear, with the exception of:

A. DISC1
B. COMT
C. RGS4
D. GRM3
E. G72

10. What percentage of first-degree relatives of schizophrenic subjects show smooth pursuit eye movement dysfunction?

A. 5-10%
B. 25-45%
C. 50-60%
D. 55-75%
E. 75-90%

11. Deficits in sensory motor gating have been used as candidate endophenotype for which of the following diseases?

A. Schizophrenia
B. Bipolar affective disorder
C. PTSD
D. Alzheimer's
E. Huntington's Chorea

12. A mother attends your clinic with her 10-year-old child with complaints of sleep disturbance, repetitive movements and self-harm behaviour. The child has an abnormally short broad head, a broad nasal bridge, fleshy upper lip and unusually prominent jaw. His condition is associated with which one of the following chromosomes?

A. Chromosome 12
B. Chromosome 13

C. Chromosome 14
D. Chromosome 17
E. Chromosome 21

13. Paternal micro deletion at chromosome 15 is associated with which of the following diseases?

A. Wilson's disease
B. Prader- Willi
C. Angelman's
D. Tuberous Sclerosis II
E. Patau's syndrome

14. Which of the following statements about endophenotypes is true?

A. They are sometimes referred to as phenotypes
B. An endophenotype cannot be neuropsychological in nature
C. They are also referred to as genotypes
D. Endophenotypes are measurable components unseen by the unaided eye along the pathway between disease and distal genotype
E. Endophenotypes can be neurophysiological but not cognitive in nature

15. Structural variation in large-scale brain systems related to motor inhibitory control may mediate genetic risk for which of the following disorders?

A. Obsessive Compulsive Disorder
B. Anorexia nervosa
C. Schizophrenia
D. Bipolar Affective Disorder
E. Depression

16. What percentage of patients suffering from dementia of Alzheimer's type (DAT) has a positive family history of DAT?

A. 10%
B. 20%
C. 25%
D. 40%
E. 60%

17. The suggested characteristics of a potentially valuable endophenotype include the following, except:

A. It can be measured before the explicit onset of the symptoms
B. It should have good reliability in the measurement of psychiatric symptomatology
C. It should be sensitive to genetic susceptibility
D. It should be specific to the disorder in question
E. It does not represent the genetic liability of non-affected relatives of probands with the disorder

18. Performance on working memory task has been identified as a reproducible candidate endophenotype for which of the following disorders?

A. Alzheimer's
B. Lewy body dementia
C. Huntington's
D. Schizophrenia
E. Parkinson's

19. D4 receptor gene has been associated with which of the following childhood disorders?

A. Childhood schizophrenia
B. ADHD
C. ASD
D. Conduct disorder
E. Down syndrome

20. An 8-year-old child attends your clinic with his mother. The child has recently started exhibiting self-injurious behaviour in the form of self-biting and hitting head against objects. Mother also reports poor concentration, impulsiveness and hyperactivity. You notice that the child has a round full face, widely spread eyes, epicanthic folds and his ears are positioned low on the head. Which of the following chromosomes is most likely to be associated with his condition?

A. Chromosome 3
B. Chromosome 5
C. Chromosome 7

D. Chromosome 13
E. Chromosome 15

21. An 11-year-old boy is referred to your clinic for assessment of ADHD. The child suffers from a rare genetic disorder and has mild learning difficulties. The child has distinctive facial features and is rather overfriendly. On your assessment you find out that not only does he seem to meet the clinical criteria for ADHD but he also has a specific phobia of fear of loud noises. The child's condition is most likely to be associated with which one of the following chromosomes?

A. Chromosome 3
B. Chromosome 4
C. Chromosome 5
D. Chromosome 6
E. Chromosome 7

22. cM Density genome-wide scan and fine mapping of chromosomal candidate regions suggest that a gene located on chromosome 10q21.3-10q22.3 is underlying the susceptibility both for schizophrenia and for bipolar disorder in which of the following population?

A. Native American population
B. Ashkenazi Jewish population
C. African American population
D. Native Dutch population
E. Chinese population

23. Pituitary adenylate cyclase-activating polypeptide (PACAP, ADCYAP1: adenylate cyclase-activating polypeptide 1), with neurotransmission modulating activity, has been suggested as a candidate gene for which of the following disorders?

A. Schizophrenia
B. Bipolar affective disorder
C. Obsessive compulsive disorder
D. Alzheimer's
E. PTSD

24. A child with mild learning disability and history of generalised seizures presents in your clinic with increasing behavioural problems of sudden rage, aggression and self-harm. He appears to have some features of ADHD. On physical examination you notice areas of thick leathery, pebbly skin on his lower back. Which of the following chromosomes is likely to be associated with his primary condition?

A. Chromosome 8
B. Chromosome 9
C. Chromosome 10
D. Chromosome 11
E. Chromosome 18

25. Which one of the following disorders is caused by deletion or disruption of a gene located on the long arm of chromosome 15 (15q11-15q13)?

A. Williams syndrome
B. ASD
C. Wilson's disease
D. Patau's syndrome
E. Angelman syndrome

26. What percentage of individuals whose clinical presentation is characteristic of Angelman syndrome show no defects on genetic laboratory studies of chromosomes 15?

A. 10%
B. 20%
C. 30%
D. 40%
E. 50%

27. Genome wide linkage scan suggest that chromosome 15q might contain genes that contribute to susceptibility to which of the following disorders?

A. Bulimia nervosa
B. Schizoaffective disorder
C. Major Depressive Disorder
D. Organic Psychosis
E. Schizophrenia

28. The genetic and environmental risk factors predisposing to externalising disorders are likely to play apart in which of the following disorders?

A. Major depression
B. Animal phobia
C. Generalised anxiety disorder
D. Conduct disorder
E. Situational phobia

29. Phosphodiesterase genes (PDE11A) have been shown to be associated with susceptibility to which of the following disorders?

A. Schizophrenia
B. Alzheimer's
C. Major Depressive Disorder
D. Simple phobia
E. PTSD

30. Recent research replicating the findings of previous studies suggests an involvement of variation at the FAT gene in the aetiology of which disorder?

A. Schizophrenia
B. BPAD
C. Recurrent Depressive Disorder
D. Schizoaffective Disorder
E. Atypical Bulimia nervosa

31. When the FMR1 gene located in the long arm of the X chromosome is switched off, it results in which of the following disorders?

A. Aicardi syndrome
B. Fragile X syndrome
C. Hunter syndrome
D. Turner's syndrome
E. Sturge-Weber syndrome

32. The risk of developing major depressive disorder among 22q11 deletion syndrome patients is:

A. 1 in 2
B. 1 in 4
C. 1 in 6
D. 1 in 8
E. 1 in 10

33. Abnormal protein 'PrPSc' produced by the PRNP gene on chromosome 20 causes which of the following diseases?

A. Huntington disease
B. Variant Creutzfeldt-Jakob (CJD) disease
C. Genetic Creutzfeldt-Jakob (CJD) disease
D. Smith-Magenis syndrome
E. Neurofibromatosis

34. DTNBP1 gene, suggested as a schizophrenia susceptibility gene, is located on which one of the following chromosomes?

A. Chromosome 2
B. Chromosome 3
C. Chromosome 4
D. Chromosome 5
E. Chromosome 6

35. Reduced caeruloplasmin is seen in a rare genetic disease, which is mapped to the long arm of which chromosome?

A. Chromosome 2
B. Chromosome 3
C. Chromosome 10
D. Chromosome 13
E. Chromosome 14

Chapter 8 - Genetics – answers

1. **B**

2. **A** – Rett syndrome is caused by mutations in the MECP2 gene found on the X chromosome. It is a childhood neurodevelopmental disorder characterised by normal early development (6-18 months) followed by loss of purposeful use of the hands, distinctive hand movements, slowed brain and head growth, gait abnormalities, seizures, and mental retardation. It affects females almost exclusively. Males can have this defect but usually don't survive to develop the syndrome. Although it is a genetic syndrome, inheritance is less than 1%. The survival is usually into middle age and beyond.

   NINDS fact sheet.

3. **B** – alpha-synuclein has been found in the filamentous inclusions in Parkinson's disease, dementia with Lewy bodies and multiple system atrophy. However, mutation in the alpha-synuclein gene is seen mainly in familial Parkinson's disease.

   Spillantini, M G: The alpha-synucleinopathies: Parkinson's disease, dementia with Lewy bodies, and multiple system atrophy. *Ann NY Acad Sci* 920: 16-27. 2000.

4. **D** – This is the chance of a child developing any psychiatric disorder and not just bipolar affective disorder. The genetic liability appears shared for bipolar affective disorder, schizoaffective disorder and schizophrenia.

   Semple, D, *et al.*: *Oxford Handbook of Psychiatry*. 2005.

5. **A**

   Duan, *et al.*: [? TITLE OF ARTICLE ?]*Cell* 130, 1- 13. 21 September, 2007.

6. **C** – Huntington's disease is a genetic disease with autosomal dominant inheritance. The genetic defect is trinucleotide repeat of CAG, between 37 and 120 repeats on chromosome 4. The classic triad is chorea, dementia and a family history. Onset is usually in 3rd and 4th decade and has a deteriorating course to death within 10-12 years. Psychiatric illnesses occur in 60-75% of patients and include anxiety, depression, psychosis and

dementia. Unfortunately, there is no treatment available to arrest the course of the disease. The penetrance is 100% with 50% risk of developing the disease in the offspring.

7. C – In the past Progranulin (PRGN) has been studied for its role in wound repair and inflammation in the periphery. However, recent research has discovered mutations in PRGN for the first time in humans to be associated with frontotemporal lobe degeneration producing frontotemporal dementia.

    Zeshan, Ahmed, *et a.l*: Progranulin in frontotemporal lobar degeneration and neuroinflammation. *Journal of Neuroinflammation* 4: 7. 2007.

8. C – While relatives of bipolar disorder (BD) probands are at increased risk of MDD, the reverse is not the case.

    Maier, *et al.*: 1992; McGuffin, *et al.*, 2003.

9. B

    Harrison, P J, *et al.*: Schizophrenia genes, gene expression, and neuropathology. *Mol Psychiatry* 10(1): 40-68. Jan 2005.

10. B – Smooth eye pursuit movement dysfunction is seen in 40-80% of schizophrenic subjects, 25-45% of their first-degree relatives and less than 10% of healthy comparison subjects.

    Irving I Gottesman, *et al.*: The Endophenotype Concept in Psychiatry. *Am J Psychiatry* 160: 636-645. April 2003.

11. A

    Irving I Gottesman, *et al.*: The Endophenotype Concept in Psychiatry. *Am J Psychiatry* 160: 636-645. April 2003.

12. D – The child has Smith-Magenis syndrome; it occurs when there is a missing piece of chromosome on the short arm of chromosome 17 (17p11.2). Smith-Magenis syndrome is characterised by particular facial features, developmental delays, mental retardation and behavioural abnormalities. The facial features include a broad square-shaped face, an abnormally short, broad head (brachycephaly); an abnormally broad, flat midface; a broad nasal bridge; an unusually prominent jaw (prognathism); eyebrows growing across the base of the nose (synophrys); a short full-tipped nose and fleshy upper lip with a tented appearance.

Developmental delays and intelligence are variable, but most affected individuals have mild to moderate mental retardation. Behavioural abnormalities include sleep disturbances, repetitive movements (stereotypy's) and a tendency to inflict harm on oneself (onychotillomania and polyembolokoilamania).

National Organisation for Rare Disorders. 2005.

13. **B** – Prader-Willi syndrome is a genetic disorder characterised by hypotonia, short stature, genital abnormalities and an excessive appetite. Patients also have some cognitive impairment that ranges from borderline normal with learning disabilities to mild mental retardation. Behavioural and psychiatric problems are common and include emotional instability, temper tantrums, obsessive/compulsive behaviour, and skin picking.

14. **D** – An endophenotype is a heritable characteristic associated with a condition, but not a direct symptom of that condition. These heritable characteristics are present in unaffected family members too. They are measurable components unseen by the unaided eye along the pathway between disease and distal genotype. An endophenotype may be neurophysiological, biochemical, endocrinological, neuroanatomical, cognitive, or neuropsychological (including configured self-report data) in nature. They are sometimes also referred to as intermediate phenotypes, but are different from phenotypes.

Tyrone D Cannon, Matthew C Keller: Endophenotypes in the Genetic Analyses of Mental Disorders. *Annual Review of Clinical Psychology*.Vol. 2, pages 267-290. April 2006.

Irving I Gottesman, *et al*.: The Endophentype Concept in Psychiatry. *Am J Psychiatry* 160: 636-645. April 2003.

15. **A** – Menies *et al*. investigated endophenotypes in OCD by measuring brain structure using magnetic resonance imaging (MRI), and behavioural performance on a response inhibition task (Stop-Signal) in 31 OCD patients, 31 of their unaffected first-degree relatives, and 31 unrelated matched controls. Both patients and relatives had delayed response inhibition on the Stop-Signal task compared with healthy controls. They used a multivoxel analysis method (partial least squares) to identify large-scale brain systems in which anatomical variation was associated with variation in performance on the response inhibition task. Behavioural

impairment on the Stop-Signal task, occurring predominantly in patients and relatives, was significantly associated with reduced grey matter in orbitofrontal and right inferior frontal regions and increased grey matter in cingulate, parietal and striatal regions, supporting the candidacy of these brain structural systems as endophenotypes of OCD.

Lara Menies, *et al.*: Neurocognitive endophenotypes of obsessive-compulsive disorder. *Brain* doi: 10.1093/brain/awm205. Sept 2007.

16. **D**

17. **E** – One of the crucial characteristics of any endophenotype described by the researchers is its ability to represent the genetic liability of non-affected relatives of probands with the disorder.

David H Skuse: *The British Journal of Psychiatry* 178: 395-396. 2001.

18. **D** – Post-mortem studies and family and twin studies have suggested heritability of working memory deficits in schizophrenia.

Gasperoni, T L, *et al.*: Genetic linkage and association between chromosome 1q and working memory function in schizophrenia. *Am J Med Genet* 116 (1 suppl): 8–16. 2003.

19. **B** – Other genes which have been associated with ADHD more recently are dopamine receptor DRD5 gene and SNAP-25 gene.

Thapar, A, *et al.*: Gene–environment interplay in attention-deficit hyperactivity disorder and the importance of a developmental perspective. *BJP* 190: 1-3. 2007.

20. **B** – The child is suffering from Cri-du-chat syndrome. CDCS is a relatively rare chromosome disorder affecting approximately 1 in 37,000-50,000 live births. The syndrome is known to result from a deletion from the short arm of chromosome 5 and represents one of the most common deletion syndromes in humans. Recent molecular research has further highlighted a 'critical region' on chromosome 5 (5p15.2). At birth, the main clinical diagnostic feature of the syndrome is a high-pitched, monochromatic 'cat-like' cry that is always present in the newborn but may disappear with age. Other features include a round, full face ('moon face'), widely spread eyes (hypertelorism), an extra fold of skin at the inner corners of the eyes (epicanthal folds), a flattened and widened nasal bridge, and ears that are positioned low on the

head. Most children with CDCS will have feeding problems from birth, including failure to thrive, poor sucking and slow weight gain. Other features include poor concentration, impulsiveness, hyperactivity, compulsive and self-injurious behaviour. They often have motor difficulties and usually have delayed milestones.

21. **E** – The child has Williams syndrome, which is caused by a micro-deletion of chromosome 7. Williams syndrome (WS) is a rare genetic disorder characterised by mild to moderate mental retardation or learning difficulties, a distinctive facial appearance, and a unique personality that combines overfriendliness and high levels of empathy with anxiety. More than 50% of children with WS have attention deficit disorders (ADD or ADHD), and about 50% have specific phobias, such as a fear of loud noises. The course and prognosis is variable depending on the degree of mental retardation.

22. **B** – Venkon, *et al.* studied 10 Belgian multigenerational families with bipolar disorder. The study also defined the chromosomal candidate region of 19.2 cM. This region has also been reported previously as a candidate region for BP disorder in several independent linkage analysis studies and in one large meta-analysis. Strongest association was seen among large Ashkenazi Jewish pedigree.

T Venkon, *et al.*: *Molecular Psychiatry* 13, 442-450. 2008

23. **A** – Research studying the effects of the associated polymorphism in the PACAP gene on neurobiological traits related to risk for schizophrenia suggests that the PACAP gene, which is over-represented in schizophrenia patients, is associated with reduced hippocampal volume and poorer memory performance. Abnormal behaviours in PACAP knockout mice, including elevated locomotor activity and deficits in prepulse inhibition of the startle response, were reversed by treatment with an atypical antipsychotic, risperidone. These convergent data suggest that alterations in PACAP signalling might contribute to the pathogenesis of schizophrenia.

R Hashimoto, *et al.*: Pituitary adenylate cyclase-activating polypeptide is associated with schizophrenia. *Molecular Psychiatry* 12, 1026.1032. 2007.

24. **B** – The child has Tuberous Sclerosis Complex (TSC). TSC is caused by defects, or mutations, on one of the two genes TSC1

and TSC2. The TSC1 gene is on the long arm of chromosome 9. The TSC2 gene is on the short arm of chromosome 16. Although some individuals inherit the disorder from a parent with TSC, most cases occur as sporadic cases due to new, spontaneous mutations in TSC1 or TSC2. In familial cases, TSC is an autosomal dominant disorder. TSC can affect many different systems of the body. Common symptoms include benign tumours, seizures, mental retardation, behaviour problems, and skin abnormalities. Behaviour problems, self-harm, aggression, ADHD and OCD often occur in children with TSC. Skin lesions include thick leathery, pebbly patches (shagreen patches), café au lait spots, adenoma sebaceum and ash leaf spots.

25. E – Angelman syndrome is a genetic disorder that causes developmental delay and neurological problems. Infants with Angelman syndrome appear normal at birth, but often have feeding problems in the first months of life and exhibit noticeable developmental delays by 6 to 12 months. They have flat heads and protruding tongues. Seizures often begin between 2 and 3 years of age. Speech impairment is pronounced, with little to no use of words. Individuals with this syndrome often display hyperactivity, jerky movements, bouts of uncontrollable laughter, sleep disorders, and movement and balance disorders that can cause severe functional deficits.

26. B – The diagnosis of Angelman syndrome is currently a clinical diagnosis which can be confirmed by genetic laboratory studies in 80% of the cases. The other 20% of cases are termed 'nondeletion, nondisomy type'. Some case reports have also suggested a link with chromosome 22q.

27. C

Peter Holmans, *et al.*: Genetics of Recurrent Early-Onset Major Depression (GenRED): Final Genome Scan Report. *Am J Psychiatry* 164: 248-258. February 2007.

28. D – The rest of the disorders come under the category of 'internalising disorders'. Shared environmental risk factors are also more pronounced for adult antisocial behaviour.

Kenneth, S: The Structure of Genetic and Environmental Risk Factors for Common Psychiatric and Substance Use Disorders in Men and Women. *Arch Gen Psychiatry* 60: 929-937. 2003.

29. C

Ma-Li Wong, *et al.*: Phosphodiesterase genes are associated with susceptibility to major depression and antidepressant treatment response. *PNAS* 10, vol. 103: 41. 2006.

30. B – A recent study suggested that the cadherin gene FAT exerts an influence on susceptibility to bipolar affective disorder (BPAD). R Abou Jarma, *et al.* aimed to replicate this finding in a German sample (425 BPAD I and 419 controls). No significant association was observed for SNPs located in the MTNR1A gene. In FAT, however, nine SNPs showed association, eight of them being located in the same haplotype block found to be associated with BPAD by Blair, *et al.*

R Abou Jarma, *et al.*: Genetic variation of the FAT gene at 4q35 is associated with bipolar affective disorder. *Molecular Psychiatry* 13, 277-284. 2008.

31. B – Fragile X is caused when there is a change, or mutation, in a single gene called the Fragile X Mental Retardation 1 (FMR1) gene, located on the long arm of the X chromosome. Fragile X syndrome is the most common inherited cause of LD, affecting 1:4,000 males and 1:8,000 females. Clinical features involve intellectual disabilities ranging from mild to profound learning disabilities. They may have long ears, faces, and jaws, loose flexible joints and flat feet. Most children with Fragile X have some behaviour challenges similar to those seen in ADHD and autism. Most boys with Fragile X have some problems with speech and language. Girls usually do not have severe problems with speech or language.

32. C – 22q11 deletion syndrome is also known as Digeorge or velocardiofacial syndrome. It is a relatively common genetic disorder causing malformations of the heart, face and limbs. Patients are at significant risk of developing psychiatric disorders.

Maynard, T M, Haskell, G T, Lieberman, J A, *et al.*: 22q11DS: genomic mechanisms and gene function in DiGeorge/velocardiofacialsyndrome. *International Journal of Developmental Neuroscience* 20, 407-419. 2002.

33. C – CJD is a progressive and fatal neurological disease. There are usually verbal and visual memory impairments with executive dysfunction and moderate to severe cognitive decline. Genetic CJD is very rare and, in the UK, on average 3 people die annually from this disease. Variant CJD is related to BSE in cattle (mad cow disease). It typically presents with psychiatric and behavioural symptoms like anxiety, depression, social withdrawal; and patients may also develop delusions and hallucinations.

R J Cordery, *et al.*: *Journal of Neurology, Neurosurgery and Psychiatry* 76: 330-336. 2005.

34. E – Chromosome 6p24-22.

N M Williams, *et al.*: Schizophrenia Bulletin 31(4): 800-805. 2005

35. D – Wilson's disease involves an abnormality of copper metabolism resulting in raised serum/urine copper and reduced caeruloplasmin. Psychiatric disorders associated with Wilson's disease are commonly mood disorders, subcortical dementia (25%) and rarely psychosis.

Chapter 9 - Epidemiology - questions

1. Which of the following statements about the incidence of a disease is true?

A. It is a measure of the risk of developing some new condition within a specified period of time
B. It is better to analyse incidence than prevalence, when studying aetiology of a disease
C. It includes morbidity and mortality rate
D. It is calculated by dividing the total number of cases over the given time period by the total population at risk during the same time period
E. It includes only individuals free of the disease who are at risk of becoming new cases

2. The estimated prevalence of postpartum blues is:

A. 5%
B. 10%
C. 15%
D. 35%
E. 60%

3. The prevalence of clinical depression after a stroke is:

A. 10 to 15%
B. 15 to 20%
C. 20 to 30%
D. 40 to 60%
E. 70 to 80%

4. Which of the following statements is not true regarding the epidemiology of schizophrenia?

A. Schizophrenia occurs equally in males and females
B. Males tend to have an earlier onset than females
C. The incidence in the UK is around 15 new cases per 100,000 population
D. Active psychosis is ranked as the second most disabling condition after dementia
E. The life-time risk of schizophrenia is between 7 and 13 per 1,000 population

5. The prevalence of obsessive compulsive disorder in the general population is:

A. 0.5-2%
B. 2-5%
C. 5-10%
D. 10-15%
E. 15-20%

6. The prevalence of substance abuse disorders is approximately:

A. 3.2%
B. 5.4%
C. 8.5%
D. 10.5%
E. 16.4%

7. All of the following statements about the General Health Questionnaire (GHQ) are true, except:

A. In epidemiological studies, a 28-items version is used
B. It is a widely used questionnaire to assess general well-being and distress
C. It was developed by Sir David Goldberg
D. 12- and 30-items versions are also available
E. It screens for non-psychotic psychiatric disorders

8. The incidence of Anorexia nervosa in adolescents and young women is approximately:

A. 0.5%
B. 2%
C. 3%
D. 5%
E. 10%

9. The incidence of ADHD in the UK is reported as:

A. 1%
B. 3%
C. 5%
D. 7%
E. 10%

10. The following statements are true according to the European Study of the Epidemiology of Mental Disorders (ESEMeD), except:

A. 12 months prevalence of major depression in the community is 5-8%
B. Life-time risk for dysthymia is 4%
C. Mean age of onset of major depression is about 27 years
D. Major depression has high co-morbidity with substance misuse
E. Rates of dystyhmia are greater in women and the divorced, the same as with major depression

11. The prevalence of epilepsy is:

A. 1%
B. 3%
C. 5%
D. 10%
E. 15%

12. What is the percentage of patients with Alzheimer's disease who have a positive family history of Alzheimer's?

A. 10%
B. 20%
C. 30%
D. 40%
E. 60%

13. Which one of the following statements about Edinburgh Postnatal Depression Scale (EPDS) is not true?

A. It is a self-rated questionnaire
B. The scale will not detect mothers with anxiety neuroses, phobias or personality disorders
C. The scale indicates how the mother has felt during the previous week
D. It is a valuable and efficient way of diagnosing 'perinatal' depression
E. Mothers who score above 13 are likely to be suffering from a depressive illness

14. What percentage of Creutzfeldt-Jakob disease results from genetic mutation?

A. 10%
B. 20%
C. 30%
D. 40%
E. 50%

15. The percentage of patients that die or become disabled within 5 years of onset of Parkinson's disease is:

A. 5%
B. 10%
C. 15%
D. 25%
E. 40%

16. The following statements regarding Patient Health Questionnaire - 9 are true, except:

A. It is a self-rated questionnaire
B. It is a depression scale used in primary care
C. It is directly based on the diagnostic criteria for major depressive disorder in ICD-10
D. It delivers a severity score to help select and monitor treatment
E. Scores of 15-19 show moderate severity of the depression

17. The approximate percentage of patients with schizophrenia that commit suicide is:

A. 2-10%
B. 5-10%
C. 10-40%
D. 30-50%
E. 40-60%

18. In patients with mood disorder, the life-time risk for suicide is:

A. 1-2%
B. 2-5%
C. 10-15%

D. 20-30%
E. 30-35%

19. The following statements regarding schizophrenia and schizophrenia-like psychosis are true, except:

A. The morbid risk of schizophrenia in first-degree relatives is 10% in late-onset schizophrenia
B. There is increased risk in both first and second generation migrants
C. Females are likely to have six-fold increased risk of developing very late-onset schizophrenia, as compared to males
D. Black and other minority ethnic groups have increased incidence of schizophrenia and other psychosis
E. There is a two-fold increase in the standardised mortality rate (SMR) in patients with schizophrenia

20. The risk of suicide in patients with HIV increases by:

A. 5x
B. 10x
C. 15x
D. 30x
E. 60x

21. Which of the following statements is not true regarding suicidal acts among depressed men and women?

A. Family history of suicide acts doubles the risk of future suicidal acts in men
B. For women, the risk for future suicidal acts is six-fold greater for prior suicide attempters
C. Early parental separation triples the risk of future suicide acts in men
D. Each past suicide attempt increases future risk by three-fold in women
E. Past drug use and cigarette smoking are associated with three-fold risk of future suicidal acts in men

22. The risk factors for Alzheimer's disease include the following, except:

A. Down's syndrome
B. Hypothyroidism
C. Previous head injury
D. Smoking
E. Parkinson's disease

23. Male to female ratio in depression is:

A. 1:1
B. 1:2
C. 1:3
D. 1:4
E. 1:5

24. Male to female ratio in hyperventilation syndrome is:

A. 1:2
B. 1:3
C. 1:5
D. 1:7
E. 1:9

25. The most common cause of premature death in schizophrenia is:

A. Heart diseases
B. Suicide
C. Substance misuse
D. Liver failure
E. Accidents

26. The following are risk factors for having depression, except:

A. Lack of parental care
B. Parental antisocial traits
C. Being married
D. Childhood sexual abuse
E. Obsessionality

27. The prevalence of cyclothymia in the general population is:

A. 1-2%
B. 3-6%

C. 8-10%
D. 10-12%
E. 12-15%

28. The mean age for developing obsessive compulsive disorder is:

A. 10 yrs
B. 15 yrs
C. 20 yrs
D. 25 yrs
E. 35 yrs

29. The risk of developing PTSD after a traumatic event for women is:

A. 2-5%
B. 5-10%
C. 10-20%
D. 20-30%
E. 30-40%

30. The male to female sex ratio in anorexia nervosa is approximately:

A. 1:2
B. 1:3
C. 1:5
D. 1:10
E. 1:15

31. Any medical ethical dilemma can be analysed with reference to the following principles, except:

A. Respect for autonomy
B. Rejection
C. Justice
D. Beneficence
E. Non-maleficence

32. Potential confounders associated with outcome in studies of major depression in those adults who experienced child sexual abuse include all of the following, except:

A. Female gender
B. Alcohol dependency
C. Parental divorce
D. No qualifications
E. Deliberate self-harm

33. Which one of the following statements is not true about the Hamilton Rating Scale for Depression (HRSD, HAM-D)?

A. It is a 17-21-item observer-rated scale
B. A score of 13 is generally regarded as indicative of a diagnosis of depression
C. Gold standard of depression rating scales
D. It is oversensitive in patients with ill physical condition who will rate more severely on this rating scale
E. It takes nearly 30 minutes to administer

34. Which one of the following statements about Kiddie-SADS-Lifetime Version (K-SADS-PL) is not correct?

A. It is a semi-structured diagnostic interview
B. It is suitable for children and adolescents from 11-18 years of age
C. It is administered by interviewing the parent(s), the child, and finally achieving summary ratings which include all sources of information
D. The Children's Global Assessment Scale (C-GAS) is completed as part of the diagnostic interview
E. If there is no evidence of current or past psychopathology, then only a screen interview is necessary to complete

35. All of the following findings were observed in a UK-wide cross-sectional survey on psychiatric morbidity and social functioning among adults with borderline intelligence living in private households, except:

A. Significant increase in psychotic disorders
B. One-eighth of the population had DSM-IV borderline intelligence
C. Increased rates of neurotic disorders, substance misuse and personality disorders
D. They were more likely to use emergency services
E. They were more likely to receive psychiatric medication, but not talking therapies

Chapter 10 – Epidemiology – answers

1. **D** – Incidence of a disease is calculated by dividing the number of new cases over the given time period by the total population at risk during the same time period.

2. **D** – The estimated prevalence of postpartum blues as shown by different studies range from 20% to 40%.

3. **D** – Depression is the most common psychiatric disorder associated with cerebrovascular disease.

4. **D** – Active psychosis is ranked as the third-most-disabling condition after quadriplegia and dementia.

   Ustun TB; Rehm J, Chatterji S, Saxena S, Trotter R, Room R, Bickenbach J, and the WHO/NIH Joint Project CAR Study Group (1999). "Multiple-informant ranking of the disabling effects of different health conditions in 14 countries". The Lancet 354 (9173): 111–15

5. **A**

   Semple et al: Oxford handbook of Psychiatry 2005

6. **E** – Data derived from multiple community surveys.

   Semple et al: Oxford handbook of Psychiatry 2005

7. **A** – In epidemiological studies, 12-items version is used. The General Health Questionnaire (GHQ) screens for non-psychotic psychiatric disorders and is available in the following versions:
   GHQ-60: the fully detailed 60-item questionnaire
   GHQ-30: a short form without items relating to physical illness
   GHQ-28: a 28 item scaled version Â– assesses somatic symptom, anxiety and insomnia, social dysfunction and severe depression
   GHQ-12: a quick, reliable and sensitive short form Â– ideal for research studies.

   Goldberg DP, et al. (1978) Manual of the General Health Questionnaire, NFER Publishing, Windsor, England

   Goldberg, D. P, Gater, R, Sartorius, N., Ustun, T. B, Piccinelli, M, Gureje, O, Rutter, C. The Validity of Two Versions of the GHQ in the WHO Study of Mental Illness in General Health Care. Psychological Medicine, 1997. 27(1):191-197

8.   A

9.   A

10. D – A 12 months prevalence of major depression in the community
     is between 2 and 5 percent.
     Alonso J, Angermeyer MC, Bernert S, Bruffaerts R et al. 12-Month comorbidity
     patterns and associated factors in Europe: results from the European Study of
     the Epidemiology of Mental Disorders (ESEMeD) project. Acta Psychiatr Scand
     Suppl. 2004;(420):28-37

11. A – The prevalence of epilepsy (recurrent seizures) is 0.5-1%.
     The lifetime prevalence of experiencing a 'seizure' is about 5%.
     Between 10-50% of patients with epilepsy experience psychiatric
     symptoms

12. D

13. D – EPDS is a valuable and efficient way of identifying patients
     at risk of 'perinatal depression'. The mother is asked to check the
     response that comes closest to how she has been feeling in the last
     7 days. The mother should complete the scale herself, unless she
     has difficulty in reading or language barrier.

     K. L. Wisner, B. L. Parry, C. M. Piontek, Postpartum Depression N Engl J Med vol.
     347, No 3, , 2002, 194-199

14. A – 85% cases are spontaneous or sporadic, 10% are due to
     genetic mutation and 5% due to Iatrogenic transmission during
     transplant surgery

15. D – 60% die within 10 years and survival over 20 years is rare

16. C – PHQ-9 is based directly on the diagnostic criteria for major
     depressive disorder in the Diagnostic and Statistical Manual
     Fourth Edition (DSM-IV). The PHQ-9 is the nine item depression
     scale of the Patient Health Questionnaire. The PHQ-9 is a powerful
     tool for assisting primary care clinicians in diagnosing depression
     as well as selecting and monitoring treatment.

     Lowe B, Unutzer J, Callahan CM, Perkins AJ, Kroenke K. Monitoring depression
     treatment outcomes with the patient health questionnaire-9. Medical Care, 2004.
     42(12): 1194-201

17. **C** – According to different studies the range is 10-38%.

18. **C**

19. **C** – Females are likely to have four fold increased risk of developing very late-onset Schizophrenia, as compared to males

    Fearon P, Kirkbride JB, Dazzan P, Morgan C, Morgan K, Lloyd T, Hutchinson G, Tarrant J, Fung WLA, Holloway J, Mallett R, Harrison G, Leff J, Jones PB, Murray RM. Incidence of schizophrenia and other psychoses in ethnic minority groups: results from the MRC AESOP Study. Psychological Medicine. 2006. 26. pp.1-10

    J McGrath, S Saha, J Welham, et al. A systematic review of the incidence of schizophrenia: the distribution of rates and the influence on sex, urbanity, migrant status and methodology. BMC Medicine 2004 ;2:13

20. **D** – The most high risk time are at diagnosis, at the death of an HIV+ friend and as the physical health of the patient deteriorates.

21. **A** – Family history of suicidal acts, past drug use, cigarette smoking, borderline personality disorder, and early parental separation each are associated with more than triple the risk of future suicidal acts in men. For women, the risk for future suicidal acts is six fold greater for prior suicide attempters; each past attempt increases future risk threefold. Suicidal ideation, lethality of past attempts, hostility, subjective depressive symptoms, fewer reasons for living, co-morbid borderline personality disorder, and cigarette smoking also increase the risk of future suicidal acts for women.

    Oquendo MA, et al. Sex differences in clinical predictors of suicidal acts after major depression: a prospective study. Am J Psychiatry. 2007; 164 (1):134-41

22. **D** – Smoking is considered as a possible protective factor.

23. **B**

24. **D**

25. **B**

26. **C** – Separation and divorce are risk factors. Other risk factors include genetic heritability, loss of a parent, major life events, personality traits of neuroticism and impulsivity. Chronic, painful

and severe physical illnesses. Also remember Brown and Harris factors.

27. **B**

28. **C** – 70% develop before 25 and 15% after 35 yrs of age.

29. **D** – For men it is 8-13%. The lifetime prevalence is estimated as 7.8%. However it is important to note that cultural differences exist.

30. **D**

31. **B** – Principlism argues that any medical ethical dilemma can be analysed and discussed with references to four principles – respect for autonomy, non-maleficence, beneficence and justice.

    Kessel A S & Silverton F. Ethics and Research in psychiatry: In Prince M, Stewart R, Ford T & Hotopf M (Eds). Practical Psychiatric Epidemiology, 2003. Oxford University Press

32. **B** – Alcohol dependency is on the causal pathway rather than a true confounder. A confounder is independently associated with exposure and outcome and is not on the causal pathway between exposure and outcome. The traumatic experience of child sexual abuse is likely to lead to alcohol dependency, which in turn increases the risk for major depression.

    Price M. Statistical Methods in psychiatric epidemiology 2: an epidemiologist perspective. In Prince M, Stewart R, Ford T & Hotopf M (Eds). Practical Psychiatric Epidemiology, 2003. Oxford University Press

33. **B** – A score of 11 is generally regarded as indicative of a diagnosis of depression.

34. **B** – Schedule for Affective Disorders and Schizophrenia for School Aged Children from 6-18 Years of age. The primary diagnoses assessed with the K-SADS-PL include: Major Depression, Dysthymia, Mania, Hypomania, Cyclothymia, Bipolar Disorders, Schizoaffective Disorders, Schizophrenia, Schizophreniform Disorder, Brief Reactive Psychosis, Agoraphobia, Separation Anxiety Disorder, Avoidant Disorder of Childhood and Adolescence, Simple Phobia, Social Phobia, Overanxious Disorder, Generalized Anxiety, Obsessive Compulsive Disorder, Attention Deficit Hyperactivity Disorder, Conduct Disorder, Oppositional

Defiant Disorder, Enuresis, Encopresis, Anorexia Nervosa, Bulimia, Transient Tic Disorder, Tourette's Disorder, Chronic Motor or Vocal Tic Disorder, Alcohol Abuse, Substance Abuse, Post-Traumatic Stress Disorder, and Adjustment Disorders.

Kaufman, Birmaher, Brent, Rao & Ryan. Diagnostic Interview Kiddie-Sads-Present and Lifetime Version (K-SADS-PL) Version 1.0 of October 1996

35. A – The prevalence of psychotic disorder was not significantly increased, but the group showed significant social disadvantage and increased rates of neurotic disorders, substance misuse and personality disorders when compared with their counterparts of normal intelligence. The data (secondary analysis) from a UK-wide cross-sectional survey of 8450 adults living in private households were collected on psychiatric disorders, intellectual level, social functioning and service use.

Hassiotis A, Strydom A, Hall I. Psychiatric morbidity and social functioning among adults with borderline intelligence living in private households. Journal of Intellectual Disability Research, Volume 52, Number 2, February 2008, pp. 95-106(12)

Note: *You'll find a lot of variation in terms of incidence, prevalence, sex ratio etc in the literature with different surveys and research reporting different results. You are advised to refer to Oxford handbook of Psychiatry by Semple D et al, if there is any doubt.*

Chapter 11 - Psychopharmacology – questions

1. Which one of the following clinicians is associated with the discovery of the pharmacological properties of lithium?

A. Delay and Deniker
B. John Cade
C. Manfred Sakel
D. Cerlitti and Binni
E. Egas Moniz

2. You are seeing a patient with rapid-cycling bipolar disorder. He asked you about a recent study, in which vagus nerve stimulation showed promising results for reduction in depressive symptoms. What will you tell him about the percentage of patients who showed improvement in their depressive symptoms?

A. 25%
B. 37%
C. 47%
D. 57%
E. 87%

3. Which one of the following statements is not correct?

A. The half-life of a drug in plasma is the time taken for its concentration to fall by a half, once dosing has ceased
B. It normally takes five times the half-life for the concentration in plasma to reach steady state, when dosing with a drug begins
C. Sertraline has elimination half-life of 48 hours
D. MAOIs should not be given with SSRIs
E. The amount eliminated over time is proportional to plasma concentration, with most psychotropic drugs

4. Which one of the following statements is not correct?

A. Bioavailability is determined by two factors: absorption and distribution
B. The law of mass action states that 'the rate of a reaction is proportional to the active masses of the reacting substances'
C. Pharmacokinetics is concerned with the time course and deposition of drugs in the body

D. In first-order kinetics the rate of absorption or elimination is directly proportional to the amount of drug remaining
E. In zero-order kinetics, a fixed amount of drug is absorbed or eliminated for each unit of time independent of drug concentrations

5. All of the following drugs inhibit Cytochrome P450 enzymes moderately to strongly, except:

A. Duloxetine
B. Fluoxetine
C. Fluvoxamine
D. Paroxetine
E. Sertraline

6. Risperidone has all of the following features, except:

A. It is associated with less sedation
B. It has a first-dose hypertensive effect
C. It is a potent 5HT2 and D2 antagonist
D. It is associated with hyperprolactonemia
E. It has low incidence of EPSE

7. A 32-year-old patient with schizophrenia has had a trial of conventional and atypical antipsychotics and is now on an optimum dose of clozapine. However, he is still partially responding to clozapine. What should be the next step?

A. Olanzapine
B. Chlorpromazine
C. Amisulpride
D. Pimozide
E. Carbamezapine

8. A 24-year-old woman with depression is on tranylcypromine. Which one of the following dietary items is safe to consume?

A. Cream cheese
B. Red wine
C. Bovril
D. Beef liver
E. Banana

9. Clozapine has a strong affinity for all of the following receptors, except:

A. 5HT2
B. 5HT3
C. D2
D. D4
E. H1

10. All of the following are true for aripiprazole, except:

A. Is not associated with systematic hyperprolactonemia
B. Is a partial agonist at D2 receptors
C. Is associated with Qt prolongation
D. Is a potent antagonist at 5HT2a receptors
E. Is not associated with significant weight gain

11. For pharmacokinetics of antidepressant drugs in breast milk all of the following are true, except:

A. There is no clinical indication for women treated with selective serotonin reuptake inhibitors (SSRIs) to stop breast-feeding
B. Doxepin has a longer-acting metabolite N-desmethyldoxepin that may accumulate in infants, causing severe drowsiness and respiratory depression
C. Trazodone appears to be of lower risk because only 5% passes into the milk
D. Mirtazapine, if used by breast-feeding mothers, infants should be monitored for potential side-effects
E. Paroxetine has a lower milk/plasma ratio than fluoxetine and sertraline

12. The following steps are important in the management of antipsychotic-induced akathesia, except:

A. Reduction of the antipsychotic dose or slow rate of increase
B. If step 1 is ineffective then switch to low-dose quetiapine/ olanzapine
C. If step 2 is ineffective then try an anti-muscarinic drug
D. The next step would involve the use of propranolol
E. If propranolol is ineffective then try clonidine

13. All of the following are recognised steps in the management of neuroleptic malignant syndrome (NMS), except:

A. Withdrawal of antipsychotic drug
B. Monitoring of vital capacity
C. Rehydration
D. Bromocriptine + dantrolene
E. Sedation with benzodiazepine

14. All of the following are true for pharmacodynamics, except:

A. It is the study of the mechanism of drug action
B. Drugs acting on GABA and glutamate are used in the management of epilepsy
C. Most psychoactive drugs only affect the function of specific neurotransmitters directly
D. Alteration in neurotransmitter function may be associated with side effects
E. Drugs affecting dopamine, noradrenaline and serotonin are usually used in the treatment of psychotic and affective disorders

15. All of the following are true for psychotropic drug metabolism in the elderly, except:

A. The amount of adipose tissue relative to total body weight generally will increase as a person ages
B. A reduction in hepatic clearance associated with old age will have the effect of prolonging elimination half-life
C. Pharmacokinetics for lipophilic drugs typically will be less in elderly subjects when compared to young individuals of the same gender
D. The duration of action of many lipophilic psychotropic drugs following single doses is dependent mainly on distribution rather than elimination or clearance
E. Old age may be associated with a reduced extent of drug binding to plasma protein

16. All of the following are true for chlorpromazine, except:

A. á2-adrenoceptor blockade causes hypotension
B. Sedating profile is due to á1-adrenoceptors and histamine H1 receptors blockade

C. It is a presynaptic inhibitor of dopamine reuptake
D. It antagonises muscarinic cholinergic receptors
E. It may cause agranulocytosis

17. Clinical features of serotonin syndrome include all of the following, except:

A. Myoclonus
B. Hypopyrexia
C. Seizures
D. Cardiac arrhythmias
E. Confusion

18. All of the following are true for the management of common adverse effects of clozapine, except:

A. Sedation smaller dose in the morning
B. Hypersalivation use of hyoscine
C. In case of seizures consider prophylactic carbamezapine
D. Constipation high-fibre diet and bulk-forming and stimulant laxatives
E. Neutropenia/agranulocytosis stop clozapine and admit to hospital

19. All of the following drugs inhibit CYP3A4 and increase carbamezapine plasma levels, except:

A. SSRIs
B. Erythromycin
C. Methadone
D. Cimetidine
E. Verapamil

20. All of the following are true for the effects of psychotropics on seizure duration during ECT, except:
A. Benzodiazepine reduces duration
B. Lithium possible increase in duration
C. MAOIs increases duration
D. Venlafaxine minimal effect
E. Anticonvulsants reduces duration

21. All of the following are true for dopamine receptors, except:

A. Five dopamine (DA) receptors have been identified
B. D1 and D5 receptors are positively coupled to cAMP
C. D2, D3 and D4 inhibit cAMP
D. D1 receptor is found both presynaptically and at post-synaptic sites
E. D1 and D2 receptors have wide distribution (striatal, mesolimbic and hypothalamic)

22. All of the following are true for recommended doses of antidepressants, except:

A. Duloxetine 60-120mg/day
B. Mirtazepine 15-45mg/day
C. Trazadone 100-200mg/day
D. Venlafaxine 75-375mg/day
E. Reboxetine 4-6mg b.d.

23. A 31-year-old lady with moderate depression was started on SSRI antidepressant medication. The following features are likely to respond favourably to the treatment, except:

A. Worsening of mood in the mornings
B. Weight loss
C. Guilt
D. Motor retardation
E. Early insomnia

24. The following statements are correct, except:

A. Cyproheptadine can be used to treat SSRIs associated anorgasmia
B. The combination of olanzapine and sulpride can improve mood symptoms in refractory schizophrenia
C. The use of clonidine is appropriate in the treatment of antipsychotic-induced akathesia
D. H2 antagonist, nizatidine has a significant role in the treatment of drug-induced weight gain
E. Alprostadil, a prostaglandin, is effective in psychotropic-induced erectile dysfunction

25. All of the following are true for approximate 'diazepam 10mg equivalent' doses of other benzodiazepines, except:

A. Lorazepam 1mg
B. Oxazepam 30mg
C. Clonazepam 1-2mg
D. Temazepam 10mg
E. Chlordiazepoxide 25mg

26. All of the following are lithium intoxication signs, except:

A. Delirium
B. Hyperreflexia
C. Coarse tremor
D. Dysarthria
E. Fatigue

27. A 62-year-old male patient with Parkinson's disease is on benzatropine. He may experience the following adverse effects, except:

A. Constipation
B. Blurred vision
C. Worsening of tardive dyskinesia
D. Excessive secretion of saliva
E. Hallucinations

28. All of the following are true for therapeutic index, except:

A. It is the ratio given by the toxic dose divided by the therapeutic dose
B. A high therapeutic index is preferable to a low one
C. A drug with narrow therapeutic index needs close monitoring
D. It is high for diazepam
E. It is high for lithium

29. Antidopamenergic actions of chlorpromazine may result in the following side effects, except:

A. Tardive dyskinesia
B. Parkinsonism
C. Dystonia
D. Ejaculatory dysfunction
E. Gynaecomestia

30. Fluoxetine is indicated for the treatment of all of the following, except:

A. Major depressive disorder
B. Obsessive-compulsive disorder
C. Moderate to severe bulimia nervosa
D. Generalised anxiety disorder
E. Panic disorder

31. Which one of the following SSRI has the longest half-life?

A. Citalopram
B. Sertraline
C. Fluoxetine
D. Escitalopram
E. Paroxetine

32. Duloxetine can be used as 'off label' in all of the following conditions, except:

A. Fibromyalgia
B. Stress urinary incontinence
C. Chronic pain
D. Multiple sclerosis
E. Chronic Fatigue syndrome

33. All of the following are true for SSRIs and diabetes mellitus, except:

A. SSRIs have a favourable effect on diabetic parameters in patients with type-2 diabetes
B. Citalopram has been associated with improvement in HbA1c
C. Most evidence is with fluoxetine
D. Fluoxetine's effects on insulin sensitivity are independent of its effects on weight loss
E. Also good evidence for sertraline

34. Pharmacokinetic properties of tricyclic antidepressant (TCAs) drugs include all of the following, except:

A. They are metabolised in the liver by the CYP-450 system
B. They are highly plasma protein bound

C. The half-lives range from 6 to 39 hours
D. They do not cross lipid barriers
E. Amitriptyline delays its own absorption

35. NICE recommendations about prophylaxis in bipolar disorder include all of the following, except:

A. Treatment for at least 3 years
B. Lithium, olanzapine and sodium valproate as first-line prophylactic agents
C. Chronic or recurrent depression may be treated with an SSRI or CBT in combination with a mood stabiliser or quetiapine or lamotrigine
D. SSRIs may be used in combination with a mood stabiliser to treat acute depressive episode
E. Combined lithium and valproate for the prophylaxis of rapid cyclic illness

Chapter 12- Psychopharmacology -answers:

1. **B** – Cade's name is associated with Lithium. Delay and Deniker introduced chlorpromazine as one of physical treatments in psychiatry for psychotic conditions. Same is true for Insulin coma treatment (Sakel), Electro-convulsive therapy (Cerlitti and Binni) and Frontal leucotomy (Moniz).

2. **B** – Investigating the efficacy of vagus nerve stimulation in a group of patients with treatment-resistant rapid-cycling bipolar disorder, Marangell LB et al, concluded that vagus nerve stimulation is an efficacious and well-tolerated therapy for patients with treatment-resistant rapid-cycling bipolar disorder, after a 12-month pilot study. Patients receiving the therapy showed an average 37.9% improvement in depressive symptoms and a 40.2% improvement in manic symptoms during the course of the study, and no patients withdrew due to adverse events. Rapid-cycling bipolar disorder, defined as four or more fully syndromic mood disturbances in the preceding 12 months, is associated with a relatively poor treatment response. Pharmacologic anticonvulsants have been some of the most effective treatments to date for rapid-cycling bipolar disorder, although relapse rates remain high. Vagus nerve stimulation is an alternative anticonvulsant treatment that is delivered by a small implanted pacemaker device. Vagus nerve stimulation appears to be effective for patients with treatment-resistant unipolar and bipolar depression, although, until now, it has remained untested in the rapid-cycling variant of the disease.

    Marangell LB et als. A 1-Year Pilot Study of Vagus Nerve Stimulation in Treatment-Resistant Rapid-Cycling Bipolar Disorder. J Clin Psychiatry 2008; 69: 183-189

3. **C** – Sertraline has an elimination half life of about 26 hours.

4. **A** – Bioavailability is determined by three factors, absorption, distribution and elimination.

    Anderson I M & Reid I C (2004)-Fundamentals of Clinical Psychopharmacology, 2nd edition, Taylor & Francis, Abingdon, Oxon

5. **E** – Sertraline weekly inhibits Cytochrome P450 enzymes. Duloxetine moderately inhibits it.

    Gelder M, Harrison P & Cowen P (Eds). Shorter Oxford Textbook of Psychiatry.2006, Oxford University Press, Oxford

6. **B** – Risperidone has first-dose hypotensive effect due to alpha-1 blockade and is the rational for using increasing dosage regimen for first few days in order to minimise this effect.

    Gardner DM et al. Modern antipsychotic drugs: a critical review. CMAJ 2005; 172: 1703-11

7. **C** – Amisulpride augmentation is worthwhile in patients on clozapine who are partial responders. It may also allow clozapine reduction. Other augmentation strategies include use of aripiprazole, haloperidol, sulpride, risperidone, lamotrigine and other mood stabilisers.

    Tranulis C et al. Somatic augmentation strategies in clozapine resistance – what facts? Clin Neuropharmacol 2006;29: 34-44

8. **A** – Tranylcypromine belongs to monoamine oxidase inhibitors (MAOIs).Foods high in amine precursors or exogenous amines may cause adverse reactions. The most common example is the hypertensive crisis. In particular, patients should be instructed not to take foods such as cheese (particularly strong or aged varieties), sour cream, Chianti wine, sherry, beer (including non-alcoholic beer), liqueurs, pickled herring, anchovies, caviar, liver, canned figs, dried fruits (raisins, prunes, etc.) bananas, raspberries, avocados, overripe fruit, chocolate, soy sauce, sauerkraut, the pods of broad beans (fava beans), yeast extracts, yogurt, meat extracts or meat prepared with tenderizers. All cheeses except ricotta and cream cheese should be avoided. Cheese is associated with most deaths.

    McGrath PJ et al. Tranylcypromine versus venlafaxine plus mirtazapine treatments for depression: a STAR* D report. Am J Psychiatry 2006; 163:1519-30

9. **C** – Clozapine only weekly binds to D1 and D2 receptors but has strong affinity for D4.

10. **C** – Aripiprazole is not associated with symptomatic hyperprolactinemia, significant weight gain, Qt prolongation or impaired glucose tolerance.

    Marder SR et al. Aripiprazole in the treatment of schizophrenia: safety and tolerability in short-term, placebo-controlled trials. Schizopher Res 2003;61: 123-36

11. C – Trazodone appears to be of lower risk because only 1% passes into the milk, although drowsiness and poor feeding have been reported. Data are limited to a few cases and caution is advised in use of the drug. For women taking antidepressants the treatment strategy while breast-feeding has been clearly established. Tricyclics such as amitryptyline, imipramine, nortriptyline and clomipramine are safe during breast-feeding. SSRIs such as fluoxetine, sertraline, paroxetine and citalopram are safe during breast-feeding. It is advisable to discontinue MAOIs, replacing them with a newer drug if necessary.

Kohen D. Psychotropic medication and breast-feeding. Advances in Psychiatric Treatment (2005) 11: 371-379

12. E – The Maudsley guidelines suggest an algorithm in the management of antipsychotic-induced akathesia. There are number of steps involved. If treatment with propranolol is not successful than cyproheptadine and benzodiazepine are considered before moving on to clonidine.

Taylor D, Paton C & Kerwin R (2007). The Maudsley Prescribing Giudelines, 9th edition, Informa Healthcare, London

13. B – Monitoring of pulse, temperature, respiratory rate, and blood pressure is important. Vital capacity is not routinely monitored. In some cases artificial ventilation may be required. L-dopa, apomorphine and carbamezapine have been used in NMS.

Lattanzi L et al. Subcutaneous apomorphine for neuroleptic malignant syndrome. Am J Psychiatry 2006 ; 163 : 1450-1

14. C – Most psychoactive drugs affect the function of specific neurotransmitters either directly or indirectly.

15. C – Pharmacokinetics for lipophilic drugs typically will be larger in elderly subjects when compared to young individuals of the same gender.

Von Moltke LL et al. Psychotropic Drug Metabolism in Old Age: Principles and Problems of Assessment, 2000

16. A – α1-adrenoceptor blockade causes hypotension. Muscarinic (cholinergic) M1/M2-receptors cause anticholinergic symptoms like dry mouth, blurred vision, constipation, difficulty/inability to urinate, sinus tachycardia, ECG-changes and loss of memory,

and the anticholinergic action may also attenuate extra-pyramidal side effects.

17. **B** – Hyperpyrexia is associated with serotonin syndrome. Serotonin syndrome is a potentially life-threatening adverse drug reaction that may occur following therapeutic drug use, inadvertent interactions between drugs, or the recreational use of certain drugs. A large number of drugs and drug combinations have been reported to produce serotonin syndrome, including antidepressants (SSRIs, MAOIs, TCAs, SNRIs, bupropion) antipsychotics (olanzapine, risperidone), opioids, CNS stimulants, 5HT1 agonists and some herbs.

Gillman P (2004). "Comment on: Serotonin syndrome due to co-administration of linezolid and venlafaxine.". J Antimicrob Chemother 54 (4): 844–5

Boyer EW, Shannon M (2005). "The serotonin syndrome". N. Engl. J. Med. 352 (11): 1112–20

18. **C** – After a seizure, withhold clozapine for a day, restart at reduced dose and give sodium valproate. An EEG may be required as EEG abnormalities are commonly seen in patients on clozapine.

Iqbal MM et al. Clozapine: a clinical review of adverse effects and management. Ann Clin Psychiatry 2003; 15: 33-48

19. **C** – Plasma levels of methadone may be reduced by carbamezapine. Other drugs may be affected; antipsychotics, antidepressants, benzodiazepines, some cholinesterase inhibitors, thyroxine and oestrogens. Carbamezapine is a potent inducer of hepatic cytochrome P450 enzymes and is metabolized by CYP3A4.

Spina E et al. Clinical significance of pharmacokinetic interactions between anti-epileptic and psychotropic drugs. Epelepsia 2002; 42 (Suppl 2): 37-44

20. **C** – MAOIs probably do not affect seizure duration but interactions with sympathomimetics used in anesthesia are possible and may lead to hypertensive crisis.

Bazire S. Psychtropic Drug Directory: The Professionals' Pocket Handbook and Aide Memoire. Salisbury: Fivepen, 2005.

21. **D** – D2 receptor is found both presynaptically and at post-synaptic sites. D3 and D4 are more localized receptors (mesolimbic, cortical and hippocampal) as compared to D1 and D2.

Anderson I M & Reid I C (2004)-Fundamentals of Clinical Psychopharmacology, 2nd edition, Taylor & Francis, Abingdon, Oxon

22. **C** – Recommended dose for trazadone is 150-300 mg/day. Up to 600 mg/day can be used in hospitalized patients.

23. **E** – Mid-late insomnia responds favorably. Onset of treatment response to SSRIs is not delayed in people with moderate to severe unipolar depression, with the greatest improvement in the first week and continued, but decreasing, improvements in subsequent weeks.

    Taylor MJ, Freemantle N, Geddes JR, et al. Early onset of selective serotonin reuptake inhibitor antidepressant action: systematic review and meta-analysis. Arch Gen Psychiatry 2006; 63:1217–23

24. **D** – H2 antagonist, nizatidine or famotidine are used in the treatment of drug-induced weight gain but not much positive evidence to support it. Effect if any is small.

    Appolinario JC et al. Psychotropic drugs in the treatment of obesity. What promise? CNS Drugs 2004; 18: 629-51

25. **D** – Temazepam 20 mg is equivalent to diazepam 10 mg.

26. **E** – Other signs of lithium intoxication include: blurred vision, lack of coordination, giddiness & ataxia, diarrhoea, vomiting, tinnitus and muscle weakness.

    Pharmacotherapy 23(6): 811-815, 2003. Pharmacotherapy Publications

    Křenová M & Pelclová D. A 4-year study of lithium intoxication reported to the Czech Toxicological Information Centre. Pharmacy World and Science 2006 ; 28: 5, pp. 274-277(4)

27. **D** – Anti-muscarinic drugs are useful in reducing siallorrhoea or excessive secretion of saliva. Antimuscarinic Drugs for Parkinson's disease include benzatropine, orphenadrine, procyclidine, trihexyphenidyl (formerly benzhexol) and amantidine. They work by reducing the effects of central cholinergic excess caused by lack of dopamine.
    Katzenschlager R, Sampaio C, Costa J et al Anticholinergics for symptomatic management of Parkinsons disease The Cochrane Database of Systematic Reviews 2002, Issue 3

28. **E** – It is low for lithium. A single drug can have many therapeutic indices.

29. **D** – Anti-adrenergic actions are usually responsible for ejaculatory failure.

30. **D** – Paroxetine and escitalopram are the approved SSRIs for generalized anxiety disorder.

31. **C** – Fluoxetine is unique because of its long half-life and the long half-life of its active metabolite norfluoxetine. Fluoxetine has a half-life of 2-4 days and its active metabolite, norfluoxetine, has a half-life of 4-16 days. In comparison, citalopram, escitalopram, paroxetine, and sertraline have shorter half-lives in the range of 20-35 hours, and steady-state concentrations (and therapeutic effect) are reached much more rapidly. The long half-life of fluoxetine may blunt the effects of missed doses or treatment discontinuation and makes it easier to discontinue than any of the other SSRIs. On the other hand, fluoxetine requires a much longer washout period than the other SSRIs (several weeks), particularly when switching to monoamine oxidase inhibitors (MAOIs) or TCA.

32. **D** – Duolextine is now officially approved for stress urinary incontinence in Europe but not in USA. Duloxetine is a potent inhibitor of serotonin and norepinephrine reuptake, with weak effects on dopamine reuptake. Duloxetine has no significant activity for muscarinic cholinergic, H1-histaminergic, or alpha 2-adrenergic receptors, and does not possess MAO-inhibitory activity.

Arnold LM, Lu Y, Crofford LJ et al. A double-blind, multicenter trial comparing duloxetine with placebo in the treatment of fibromyalgia patients with or without major depressive disorder. Arthritis Rheum 2004;50:2974-84

Millard RJ, Moore K, Rencken R, Yalcin I, Bump RC; Duloxetine UI Study Group. Duloxetine vs placebo in the treatment of stress urinary incontinence: a four-continent randomized clinical trial. BJU Int. 2004 ;93(3):311-8

33. **B** – Fluoxetine has been associated with improvement in HbA1c levels, reduced insulin requirements and weight loss.

Gulseren L et al. Comparasion of flouxetine and paroxetine in type 2 diabetes mellitus patients. Arch Med Res 2005; 36: 159-65

34. **D** – All TCAs are lipid soluble and hence readily cross lipid barriers such as the blood-brain barrier and placenta.

35. **A** – NICE recommends treatment for at least 2 years and longer in

high-risk patients.

National Institute for Health and Clinical Excellence. Bipolar disorder. The management of bipolar disorder in adults, children and adolescents, in primary and secondary care. Clinical guidance 38. http://www.nice.org.uk. 2006

Chapter 13 – EMIs – questions

I – Physical treatments in psychiatry

Options

A. Meduna
B. Sakle
C. Delay and Deniker
D. Cerletti and Bini
E. Takezaki and Hanaoka
F. Fernandez and Lopez-Ibor
G. Moniz
H. Cade

Lead in: From the above list, please choose names of clinicians associated with the following physical treatments in psychiatry.

Each option might be used once, more than once, or not at all.

1. Electroconvulsive therapy (choose <u>one</u> option)
2. Clomipramine in OCD (choose <u>one</u> option)
3. Chlorpromazine (choose <u>one</u> option)

II – Neurotransmitters and psychiatric disorders

Options

A. Histamine
B. 5-Hydroxytryptamine (5-HT)
C. Dopamine (DA)
D. Acetylcholine (ACh)
E. Noradrenaline (NA)
F. Gamma-aminobutyric acid (GABA)
G. Adrenaline

Lead in: For each of the following psychiatric disorders, choose the most appropriate neurotransmitters from the above options.

Each option might be used once, more than once, or not at all.

4. Alzheimer's disease (choose <u>one</u> option)
5. Schizophrenia (choose <u>three</u> options)
6. Depression (choose <u>two</u> options)

III – Antipsychotic drugs and neuroreceptors

Options

    A. D1 receptor
    B. D2 receptor
    C. D4 receptor
    D. 5 HT2
    E. 5 HT3
    F. Alpha 1 & 2 receptors

Lead in: For each of the following antipsychotic drugs, choose the most appropriate neuroreceptors from the above options.

Each option might be used once, more than once, or not at all.

    7. Haloperidol (choose <u>one</u> option)
    8. Risperidone (choose <u>two</u> options)
    9. Clozapine (choose <u>four</u> options)
    10. Olanzapine (choose <u>two</u> options)

IV – Antipsychotic drugs classification

Options

    A. Haloperidol
    B. Clozapine
    C. Risperidone
    D. Amisulpride
    E. Trifluperazine
    F. Flupenthixol
    G. Quetiapine

Lead in: Choose the appropriate antipsychotic drug from above for each of the following group.

Each option might be used once, more than once, or not at all.

11. Phenothiazine (choose <u>one</u> option)
12. Benzisoxazole (choose <u>one</u> option)
13. Dibenzodiazepines (choose <u>one</u> option)

V - SSRIs and adverse effects

Options

A. Citalopram
B. Sertraline
C. Fluoxetine
D. Paroxetine
E. Escitalopram
F. Fluvoxamine

Lead in: For each of the following adverse effect profiles, choose the most appropriate SSRIs from the above options.

Each option might be used once, more than once, or not at all.

14. Sedation, extra-pyramidal and discontinuation symptoms are more common (choose <u>one</u> option)
15. Insomnia, tremor, hyponatraemia, sexual dysfunction, dyspepsia, agitation (choose <u>three</u> options)
16. Insomnia and agitation more common. May alter insulin requirement (choose <u>one</u> option)

VI - Secondary binding properties of SSRIs

Options

A. Most selective serotonin reuptake inhibitor
B. Least selective serotonin reuptake inhibitor
C. More potent dopamine uptake inhibitor than other SSRIs
D. Most potent blocker of muscarinic receptors among the SSRIs
E. Selective serotonin and norepinephrine reuptake inhibitor

Lead in: For each of the following SSRIs, choose the most appropriate secondary binding properties from the above options.

Each option might be used once, more than once, or not at all.

17. Fluoxetine (choose <u>one</u> option)
18. Sertraline (choose <u>one</u> option)
19. Citalopram (choose <u>one</u> option)
20. Paroxetine (choose <u>one</u> option)
21. Escitalopram (choose <u>one</u> option)

VII - Cardiac effects of antidepressants

Options

A. TCAs
B. Venlafaxine
C. MAOIs
D. SSRI
E. Reboxetine
F. Duloxetine
G. Trazodone
H. Mirtazapine

Lead in: Match the most appropriate set of cardiac effects profile in each question below with the most appropriate antidepressant drug from the above options.

Each option might be used once, more than once, or not at all.

22. Reduction in heart rate, risk of hypertensive crisis and may cause cardiac arrhythmia (choose <u>one</u> option)
23. Reduction in heart rate, significant postural hypertension and can prolong QTc interval (choose <u>one</u> option)
24. Minimal effect on blood pressure, no effect on QTc interval and cardiac conduction (choose <u>one</u> option)

VIII - Use of questionnaires in psychiatric disorders

Options

A. Self rated instrument
B. Clinician-administered instrument
C. 10-items version
D. 12-items version
E. 14-items version
F. 30-items version
G. 45-items version
H. 64-items version

Lead in: For each of the following questions, choose the most appropriate options from the above list.

Each option might be used once, more than once, or not at all.

25. The Hospital Anxiety and Depression Scale (HADS) (choose two options)
26. General Health Questionnaire (GHQ) (choose three options)
27. Edinburgh Postnatal Depression Scale (EPDS) (choose two options)

IX – Depression and measuring scales

Options

A. Scores of 11-14
B. Scores of 13 and above
C. Scores of 15-21
D. Scores of 21-28
E. Scores of 29-35
F. Scores of 29-63

Lead in: For each of the following statements, choose the most appropriate score range from the above list.

Each option might be used once, more than once, or not at all.

28. Likely to be suffering from a depressive illness of varying severity using Edinburgh Postnatal Depression Scale (EPDS) (choose one option)
29. Likely to be suffering from a depressive illness of moderate severity on Hospital and Anxiety Scale (HADS) (choose one option)

30. Likely to be suffering from a depressive illness of severe severity on Becks Depression Inventory (BDI) (choose <u>one</u> option)

X - Psychiatric assessment tools

Options

   A. A self-rated tool
   B. A clinician-administered tool
   C. A 7-items scale
   D. A 9-items scale
   E. An 11-items scale
   F. A 21-items scale
   G. A 30-items instrument

Lead in: For each of the following psychiatric rating scales, choose the most appropriate options from the above list.

Each option might be used once, more than once, or not at all.

31. Young Mania Rating Scale (YMRS) (choose <u>two</u> options)
32. Positive and Negative Syndrome Scale (PANSS) (choose <u>two</u> options)
33. Calgary Depression Scale for Schizophrenia (CDSS) (choose <u>two</u> options)

XI - Advantages of analytical observational studies

Options

   A. Good for diagnosis and aetiology
   B. Can assess multiple outcome
   C. Useful for prevalence studies
   D. Suitable for rare exposures
   E. Cheap and simple
   F. Can study rare diseases
   G. Little statistical power

Lead in: For each of the following study types, choose the most appropriate advantages from the list above.

Each option might be used once, more than once, or not at all.

34. Cohort study (choose <u>two</u> options)
35. Cross-sectional survey (choose <u>two</u> options)
36. Case-control study (choose <u>two</u> options)

XII – Disadvantages of analytical observational studies

Options

A. Expensive to set up and maintain
B. Temporal relationship is difficult to establish
C. Establishes association, not causality
D. Can take a long time from exposure to the onset of the disease
E. Not suitable for rare exposures
F. Need large numbers

Lead in: For each of the following study types, choose the most appropriate disadvantages from the list above.

Each option might be used once, more than once, or not at all.

37. Cross-sectional survey (choose <u>two</u> options)
38. Cohort study (choose <u>two</u> options)
39. Case-control study (choose <u>two</u> options)

XIII – Mood stabilisers in overdose

Options

A. Gabapentin
B. Valproate
C. Carbamezapine
D. Lamotrigine
E. Lithium

Lead in: Please choose the drug from the above list which may be

responsible for the overdose in each scenario given below.
Each option might be used once, more than once, or not at all.

40. Somnolence, coma, cerebral oedema, respiratory depression, hypotension, seizures (choose <u>one</u> option)
41. Nausea, diarrhoea, tremor, confusion, lethargy, coma, cardiovascular collapse (choose <u>one</u> option)
42. Tachycardia, ataxia, somnolence, respiratory depression, seizures, electrolyte imbalance (choose <u>one</u> option)

XIV – Depression assessment tools

Options

A. Montgomery-Asberg Depression Rating Scale (MADRAS)
B. Geriatric Depression Scale
C. Hamilton Depression Rating Scale (HAM-D)
D. Beck Depression Inventory (BDI)
E. Calgary Depression Scale for Schizophrenia (CDSS)

Lead in: Please choose the appropriate depression rating scales from the above list which correctly match each description given below.

Each option might be used once, more than once, or not at all.

43. It focuses on the cognitive rather than the physical aspects of depressive illness (choose <u>one</u> option)
44. Clinician-administered scale designed to measure the treatment changes of depression (choose <u>one</u> option)
45. The scale tends to assess somatic symptoms more thoroughly, with less emphasis on affective and cognitive symptoms (choose <u>one</u> option)

XV – Measuring attitudes

Options

A. Likert scale
B. Thurstone rating scale
C. Osgood's semantic differentials

D. Guttman scale
E. Rotter's locus of control scale

Lead in: Please choose the appropriate scales from the above list for each of the descriptions given below.

Each option might be used once, more than once, or not at all.

46. Intervals between the statements are approximately equal on this scale (choose <u>one</u> option)
47. The purpose of this scale is to establish a one-dimensional continuum for a concept one wish to measure (choose <u>one</u> option)
48. This scale measures how strongly people agree/disagree with favourable/unfavourable statements (choose <u>one</u> option)

XVI – Biosynthesis of neurotransmitters

Options

A. L aromatic acid decarboxylase
B. Tyrosine hydroxylase
C. Monoamine oxidase
D. Dopamine â-hydroxylase
E. DOPA decarboxylase
F. Tryptophan hydroxylase
G. Aldehyde dehydrogenase
H. Phenyl ethanolamine N-methyl transferase

Lead in: Which of the above enzymes are used in the specific step mentioned in each question below?

Each option might be used once, more than once, or not at all.

49. Noradrenalin conversion to adrenaline (choose <u>one</u> option)
50. 5-hydroxytryptophan conversion to serotonin (choose <u>one</u> option)
51. Tyrosine conversion to dopamine (choose <u>three</u> options)
52. Serotonin conversion to 5-hydroxyindoleacetic acid (choose <u>two</u> options)

XVII – Functional roles of dopamine receptors

Options

- A. D1
- B. D2
- C. D3
- D. D4
- E. D5

Lead in: Which of the above receptors are most strongly implicated in the functions mentioned in the questions below?

Each option might be used once, more than once, or not at all.

53. Regulation of arousal and mood through cortex (choose <u>two</u> options)
54. Regulation of motor control through basal ganglia (choose <u>two</u> options)
55. Regulation of endocrine control through pituitary gland (choose <u>one</u> option)
56. Regulation of autonomic and endocrine control through hypothalamus (choose <u>two</u> options)
57. Regulation of emotions and stereotypic behaviour through limbic system (choose <u>two</u> options)

XVIII – Vertigo and lesions at neuroanatomical sites

Options

- A. Temporal lobe
- B. Frontal lobe
- C. Cerebellum
- D. Parietal lobe
- E. Occipital lobe
- F. Cerebellopontine angle
- G. Brain stem
- H. None of the above

Lead in: Which of the above neuroanatomical sites are likely to be involved in the following vignettes?

Each option might be used once, more than once, or not at all.

58. 55-year-old male presents with vertigo, facial weakness and numbness, tinnitus, hearing loss and poor co-ordination of limbs (choose <u>one</u> option)
59. 43-year-old female presents with vertigo, 'blank episodes', formed visual hallucinations and olfactory hallucinations of burning rubber (choose <u>one</u> option)
60. 59-year-old male presents with vertigo, drop attacks, dysarthria, perioral numbness and weakness and numbness of limbs (choose <u>one</u> option)
61. 62-year-old male presents with vertigo, nystagmus, lack of balance and poor co-ordination (choose <u>one</u> option)

XIX – Measures of brain activity

Options

A. Isotope required
B. Direct measure of neuronal activity
C. Good spatial resolution
D. Good temporal resolution
E. Requires averaging EEG activity
F. Dependent on level of oxygen in blood
G. Measures oxygen and glucose consumption
H. Time-locked to repeated triggers
I. P300 response

Lead in: Which of the above characteristics are most relevant to each of the following methods of measuring brain activity?

Each option might be used once, more than once, or not at all.

62. Positron emission tomography (choose <u>three</u> options)
63. Event-related potential (choose <u>three</u> options)
64. Functional magnetic resonance imaging (choose <u>two</u> options)
65. Electroencephalogram (choose <u>two</u> options)

XX – Apraxia

Options

    A. Left limb apraxia
    B. Orofacial apraxia
    C. Constructional apraxia
    D. Dressing apraxia
    E. Sympathetic apraxia of right limb
    F. Ideomotor apraxia
    G. Ideational apraxia

Lead in: Which of the above apraxias result from damage to each of the following structures?

Each option might be used once, more than once, or not at all.

    66. Anterior corpus callosum (choose <u>two</u> options)
    67. Anterior left hemisphere (choose <u>one</u> option)
    68. Right parietal lobe (choose <u>one</u> option)
    69. Left parietal lobe (choose <u>one</u> option)

XXI - Lesion localisation

Options

    A. Left frontal lobe lesion
    B. Left parietal lobe lesion
    C. Right parietal lobe lesion
    D. Left temporal lobe lesion
    E. Occipital lobe lesion
    F. Bilateral occipito-parietal lesion

Lead in: Which of the above lesions are implicated in each of the following symptoms?

Each option might be used once, more than once, or not at all.

    70. Apperceptive visual agnosia (choose <u>one</u> option)
    71. Jacksonian seizures (choose <u>one</u> option)
    72. Acalculia (choose <u>one</u> option)

XXII – Neuroimaging

Options

- A. Parkinson's disease
- B. Fahr's disease
- C. Normal pressure hydrocephalus
- D. Delirium
- E. AIDS dementia
- F. SLE
- G. Huntington's disease
- H. Wilson's disease
- I. Progressive supra nuclear palsy
- J. Pick's disease
- K. Alzheimer's dementia

Lead in: Which of the above diseases correlate to each of the following neuroimaging results?

Each option might be used once, more than once, or not at all.

73. Low-voltage and absent alpha waves on EEG (choose <u>one</u> option)
74. Ring-enhancing lesions seen on MRI scan (choose <u>one</u> option)
75. Enlarged frontal horns of lateral ventricles on CT and MRI scans (choose <u>one</u> option)

XXIII – Neuroimaging

Options

- A. Parkinson's disease
- B. Fahr's disease
- C. Normal pressure hydrocephalus
- D. Delirium
- E. AIDS dementia
- F. SLE
- G. Huntington's disease
- H. Wilson's disease
- I. Progressive supra nuclear palsy

J. Pick's disease
K. Alzheimer's dementia

Lead in: Which of the above diseases correlate to each of the following neuroimaging results?

Each option might be used once, more than once, or not at all.

76. There is a correlation between psychosis and flow to frontal lobes on SPECT scan (choose <u>one</u> option)
77. Abnormal frontotemporal theta slowing on EEG in otherwise asymptomatic patient (choose <u>one</u> option)
78. Theta and delta wave slowing on EEG with maximal abnormality in parietal lobes (choose <u>one</u> option)

XXIV - Diagnosis

Options

A. Parkinson's disease
B. Fahr's disease
C. Normal pressure hydrocephalus
D. Delirium
E. Lewy body dementia
F. SLE
G. Huntington's disease
H. Wilson's disease
I. Progressive supra nuclear palsy
J. Pick's disease
K. Alzheimer's dementia

Lead in: Which of the above diseases correlate to each of the following scenarios?

Each option might be used once, more than once, or not at all.

79. A 56-year-old female with no previous psychiatric history presents with memory problems, paranoid thinking, auditory hallucinations, clumsiness, fatigability, unsteady gait, dysphagia, under-performance on frontal lobe tests and bilateral calcification of basal ganglia (choose <u>one</u> option)

80. A 22-year-old male presents with depression and personality changes consisting of impulsivity also has tremor, rigidity, poor co-ordination, abnormal gait and dysarthria. He was found to have chronic hepatitis and haemolytic anaemia (choose <u>one</u> option)

81. A 67-year-old male presents with visual hallucinations, fluctuation of consciousness and spontaneous Parkinsonism (choose <u>one</u> option)

XXV - Gait

Options

    A. Parkinson's disease
    B. Fahr's disease
    C. Normal pressure hydrocephalus
    D. Delirium
    E. Lewy body dementia
    F. SLE
    G. Huntington's disease
    H. Wilson's disease
    I. Progressive supra nuclear palsy
    J. Pick's disease
    K. Alzheimer's dementia

Lead in: Which of the above diseases correlate to each of the following gaits?

Each option might be used once, more than once, or not at all.

82. Dancing gait (choose <u>one</u> option)
83. Magnetic gait (choose <u>one</u> option)
84. Shuffling gait (choose <u>one</u> option)

XXVI - Attachment and bonding

Options

    A. Freud
    B. Bowlby

C. Erikson
D. Lorenz
E. Winnicott
F. Piaget
G. Kohlberg
H. Thomas and Chess

Lead in: Which of the above individuals are associated with the following aspects of attachment and bonding mentioned in each question below?

Each option might be used once, more than once, or not at all.

85. Transitional object (choose <u>one</u> option)
86. Imprinting (choose <u>one</u> option)
87. Attachment theory (choose <u>one</u> option)
88. Maternal deprivation (choose <u>one</u> option)

XXVII - Temperament

Options

A. Relatively inactive
B. Irritable
C. Playful
D. Irregular eating pattern
E. Regular sleeping pattern
F. Intense negative reaction to new situation
G. Withdrawal from a new situation in a mild way
H. Regular eating pattern
I. Irregular sleeping pattern

Lead in: Which of the above features are associated with the types of temperaments described in each question below?

Each option might be used once, more than once, or not at all.

89. Easy temperament (choose <u>three</u> options)
90. Difficult temperament (choose <u>four</u> options)
91. Slow to warm up temperament (choose <u>two</u> options)

XXVIII - Adult attachment styles

Options

   A. High avoidance
   B. Low avoidance
   C. High anxiety levels
   D. Low anxiety levels
   E. Willing to rely on others
   F. Exaggerated desire for closeness and dependence
   G. High fear of rejection
   H. View close relationships as unimportant and value independence and self-reliance
   I. Comfortable with intimacy
   J. Avoid intimacy

Lead in: Which of the above features are associated with the types of attachments in adults described in each question below?
Each option might be used once, more than once, or not at all.

   92. Secure attachment (choose <u>four</u> options)
   93. Preoccupied adults (choose <u>four</u> options)

XXIX - Psychosocial influences on mental illness

Options

   A. Schizophrenia
   B. Mania
   C. Depression
   D. Anxiety
   E. Parasuicide
   F. Eating disorders
   G. Personality disorders
   H. Functional disorders

Lead in: Which of the above illnesses are more closely associated with the psychosocial factors described in each question below?

Each option might be used once, more than once, or not at all.

94. Significant life events usually precede the onset of this illness (choose <u>two</u> options)
95. Life events are more likely to occur before relapse than before the onset (choose <u>one</u> option)
96. High expressed emotions are associated with relapse (choose <u>one</u> option)
97. Threatening life events usually trigger this (choose <u>two</u> options)

XXX - Perception

Options

   A. Finger agnosia
   B. Anosogosia
   C. Prosopagnosia
   D. Astereognosia
   E. Simultanagnosia
   F. Agraphaesthesia
   G. Autotopagnosia
   H. Hemisomatognosis

Lead in: Which of the above agnosias are best described in each of the questions below?

Each option might be used once, more than once, or not at all.

98. Patient is unable to recognise parts of his own body (choose <u>one</u> option)
99. Patient is unable to recognise familiar faces (choose <u>one</u> option)
100. Patient is unable to understand the overall meaning of a picture but is able to recognise individual parts of it (choose <u>one</u> option)

XXXI - Memory

Options

   A. Episodic memory loss
   B. Fast forgetting on recall tasks
   C. Ribot's Law

D. Impaired priming
E. Semantic memory
F. Functional and structural changes in hippocampus and prefrontal cortex
G. Executive problems
H. Loss of personal identity
I. Temporary dysfunction in limbic-hippocampal circuits

Lead in: Which of the above are best associated with the memory problems described in each of the questions below?

Each option might be used once, more than once, or not at all.

101. Memory problems in PTSD (choose two options)
102. Temporally graded retrograde amnesia (choose one option)
103. Transient global amnesia (choose one option)

XXXII – Neuropsychological tests

Options

A. Stroop colour word interference test
B. Trail-making test
C. Visual search test
D. Revised token test
E. Benton verbal fluency test
F. Rey auditory verbal learning test
G. Adult memory and information processing battery
H. Dichotic listening test

Lead in: Which of the above neuropsychological tests are used to test the functions described in each of the questions below?
Each option might be used once, more than once, or not at all.

104. Laterality (choose one option)
105. Language (choose two options)
106. Memory (choose two options)
107. Information processing (choose three options)

XXXIII – Study design

Options

   A. Analytical observational study
   B. Descriptive observational study
   C. Experimental study

Lead in: Choose the most appropriate study design from the above list for each of the following studies:

Each option might be used once, more than once, or not at all.

   108. Group of patients with a diagnosis of bipolar effective disorder given lithium and then followed for 6 month to see whether they remain symptom-free (choose <u>one</u> option)
   109. Two groups of factory workers, one exposed to asbestos and the other not exposed to asbestos are followed up for 20 years to see whether they develop lung cancer (choose <u>one</u> option)
   110. A study of incidence of schizophrenia in Japan (choose <u>one</u> option)

XXXIV - Study design

Options

   A. Audit
   B. Case-control study
   C. Cohort study
   D. Randomised controlled trial
   E. Open trial
   F. Ecological study
   G. Qualitative study
   H. Pragmatic trial
   I. Cross-over trial

Lead in: Choose the most appropriate study design from the above list for each of the following studies:

Each option might be used once, more than once, or not at all.

   111. All the patients with depression from a large outpatient clinic are randomised into two groups. Group 1 is given SSRI and Group 2 is given SNRI and then followed up for 6 months to see the response (choose one option)

112. 100 patients with a diagnosis of schizophrenia are compared with 100 patients without schizophrenia by checking their birth records for obstetric complications, in order to determine any association between obstetric complications and schizophrenia (choose one option)

113. 50 patients with a diagnosis of PTSD are informed and given a new drug and then observed in the outpatient clinic for 6 months to observe the response (choose one option)

XXXV - Clinical trials

Options

A. Open trial
B. Controlled trial
C. Randomised controlled trial
D. Pragmatic trial
E. Cross-over trial
F. Cluster trial
G. N of 1 trial

Lead in: For each of the following scenarios, choose the most appropriate type of trial from the above list.

Each option might be used once, more than once, or not at all.

114. In order to compare 3 different models of medical training, 15 medical schools in the country are randomised to receive these different models, with an equal number of medical schools for each training model (choose one option)

115. In order to assess a new therapy for OCD, all the patients with OCD in your clinic are divided into two groups. One group is given the new therapy t and the other group is given CBT. The response is compared over the next 6 months (choose one option)

116. 50 patients in an eating disorder clinic are given one treatment for 3 weeks and then, after a gap of 1 week, they receive a different treatment for 3 weeks. The effects of both treatments are then compared (choose one option)

XXXVI - Reliability

Options

    A.   Inter-rater reliability
    B.   Intra-rater reliability
    C.   Test-Retest reliability
    D.   Parallel-Forms reliability
    E.   Internal consistency reliability

Lead in: For each of the following descriptions, choose the most appropriate type of reliability from the above options.

Each option might be used once, more than once, or not at all.

    117. Assesses the consistency of the results of two tests constructed in the same way from the same content (choose <u>one</u> option)
    118. Assesses the degree of agreement between assessments of 2 or more different observers (choose <u>one</u> option)
    119. Assesses the consistency of a measure from one time to another (choose <u>one</u> option)

XXXVII - Bias

Options

    A.   Berkson bias
    B.   Attrition bias
    C.   Performance bias
    D.   Diagnostic purity bias
    E.   Neyman bias
    F.   Recall bias
    G.   Hawthorne effect
    H.   Ascertainment bias
    I.   Membership bias
    J.   Diagnostic suspicion bias

Lead in: For each of the following descriptions, choose one option from the above list.

Each option might be used once, more than once, or not at all.

120. Bias arising due to a time gap between exposure and the actual selection of the study population, such that some individuals with exposure become unavailable for selection (choose <u>one</u> option)
121. Bias that refers to the systematic differences between the comparison groups in the loss of participants from the study (choose <u>one</u> option)
122. Bias due to a systematic distortion in measuring the true frequency of a phenomenon due to a distorted or non-typical sample (choose <u>one</u> option)

XXXVIII – Study interpretation

Options

A. Relative risk
B. Relative risk reduction
C. Absolute risk
D. Absolute risk reduction
E. Odds ratio
F. Numbers needed to treat

Lead in: For each of the following definitions, choose the most appropriate option from the above list.

Each option might be used once, more than once, or not at all.

123. Risk of an event in one group minus the risk in the other group (choose <u>one</u> option)
124. The difference in event rates expressed relative to the control event rate, usually expressed as a percentage (choose <u>one</u> option)
125. The difference in event rates between the experimental group and the control group, usually expressed as a percentage (choose <u>one</u> option)

XXXIX – Study interpretation

Options

A. Sensitivity

B.   Positive predictive value
C.   Negative predictive value
D.   Specificity
E.   Likelihood ratio for a positive test
F.   Likelihood ratio for a negative test

Lead in: For each of the following statements, choose the most appropriate option from the above list.

Each option might be used once, more than once, or not at all.

126. It measures the proportion of people without a disorder correctly classified by a test (choose <u>one</u> option)
127. It measures the proportion of people with a negative test that do not have the disorder (choose <u>one</u> option)
128. It measures the proportion of people with a disorder correctly classified by a test (choose <u>one</u> option)

XL – Statistical tests

Options

A.   Mcnemer's test
B.   Student's t test (paired)
C.   One-way analysis of variance
D.   Mann-Whitney U test
E.   Regression analysis
F.   Multiple regression
G.   Kruskal-Wallis ANOVA
H.   Chi-squared test

Lead in: For each of the following scenarios, choose the most appropriate parametric test from the above list.

Each option might be used once, more than once, or not at all.

129. A patient is started on beta blocker for the treatment of hypertension. The blood pressure is recorded at 1 week, 2 week, 3 week and 4 week to see if the blood pressure is reduced by the medication (choose <u>one</u> option)
130. You want to see if the blood glucose level varies with the

weight of the patient (choose <u>one</u> option)

131. You want to check if the weight of a patient increases after taking antipsychotic medication by comparing the weight before and after taking antipsychotic (choose <u>one</u> option)

XLI – Descriptive statistics

Options

    A. Mean
    B. Median
    C. Range
    D. Interquartile range
    E. Standard deviation

Lead in: For each of the following definitions, choose the most appropriate option from the above list.

Each option might be used once, more than once, or not at all.

132. It is the central value, in the middle of all values (choose <u>one</u> option)
133. It is the difference between the values that are midway between the median and the two extremes (choose <u>one</u> option)
134. It is the sum of all values divided by the number of values (choose <u>one</u> option)

XLII – Types of data

Options

    A. Categorical data
    B. Continuous data
    C. Binary data
    D. Ordinal data
    E. Nominal data
    F. Ratio data

Lead in: For each of the following, choose the most appropriate option from the above list.

Each option might be used once, more than once, or not at all.

135. Data that can have any value within the range of all possible values (choose <u>one</u> option)
136. A type of categorical data in which objects fall into unordered categories (choose <u>one</u> option)
137. Data which can only have set values (choose <u>one</u> option)

XLIII - Risk of schizophrenia in relatives

Options

    A. 0.5-1%
    B. 3%
    C. 6%
    D. 12-15%
    E. 20-30%
    F. 40%
    G. 46%
    H. 64%

Lead in: A 22-year-old female suffers from schizophrenia. What are the risks among her relatives of developing schizophrenia?

Each option might be used once, more than once, or not at all.

138. Her identical twin sister (choose <u>one</u> option)
139. Son of her daughter; her daughter does not suffer from schizophrenia (choose <u>one</u> option)
140. Her husband (choose <u>one</u> option)
141. Her son (choose <u>one</u> option)
142. Her daughter, if the father of her daughter also suffers from schizophrenia (choose <u>one</u> option)

XLIV - Genetic disorders and features

Options

    A. Chorea
    B. Cat-like cry
    C. Elfin features
    D. Pronounced speech impairment
    E. Kayser-Fleischer rings
    F. Dementia
    G. Bouts of uncontrollable laughter
    H. Fear (phobia) of loud noise
    I. Wing-beating tremor
    J. Moon face

Lead in: Choose the most appropriate associations from the above list for each of the following chromosomes.

Each option might be used once, more than once, or not at all.

   143. Long arm of chromosome 13 (choose two options)
   144. Trinucleotide repeat of CAG on chromosome 4 (choose two options)
   145. Short arm of chromosome 5 (choose two options)

XLV - Genetics and dementia of Alzheimer type (DAT)

Options

    A. Chromosome 1
    B. Chromosome 3
    C. Chromosome 9
    D. Chromosome 14
    E. Chromosome 15
    F. Chromosome 19
    G. Chromosome 21
    H. Chromosome 22

Lead in: Several genes have been implicated in the aetiology of DAT. Choose the most appropriate associations from the above list for each of the following gene/codes implicated in DAT.

Each option might be used once, more than once, or not at all.

   146. Codes for presenilin 1 (choose one option)

147. Gene for Amyloid precursor protein (APP) (choose <u>one</u> option)
148. Codes for the presenilin 11 (choose <u>one</u> option)
149. Codes for Apolipoprotein E4 (choose <u>one</u> option)

XLVI - Genetic disorders and LD

Options

A. Sex chromosome disorder
B. Autosomal dominant
C. Autosomal recessive
D. X-linked recessive
E. X-linked dominant

Lead in: For each of the following disorders, choose the most appropriate associations from the above list.

Each option might be used once, more than once, or not at all.

150. Fragile X syndrome (choose <u>one</u> option)
151. Trisomy X (choose <u>one</u> option)
152. Neurofibromatosis (choose <u>one</u> option)
153. Laurence-Moon syndrome (choose <u>one</u> option)
154. Lesch-Nyhan syndrome (choose <u>one</u> option)

XLVII - Features of genetic disorders

Options

A. Males usually don't survive to develop the syndrome
B. Excessive appetite
C. Chorea
D. Prognathism
E. Kayser-Fleischer rings
F. Slowed brain and head growth
G. Elfin features
H. Obsessive compulsive behaviour
I. Onychotillomania

Lead in: For each of the following genetic disorders, choose the most appropriate associations from the above list.

Each option might be used once, more than once, or not at all.

155. Smith–Magenis syndrome (choose <u>two</u> options)
156. Rett's syndrome (choose <u>two</u> options)
157. Prader-Willi syndrome (choose <u>two</u> options)

Chapter 14 - EMIs - answers

I.
- 1. **D**
- 2. **F**
- 3. **C**

II.
- 4. **D**
- 5. **B, C, E**
- 6. **B, E**
  Anderson, I M & Reid, I C: *Fundamentals of Clinical Psychopharmacology*, 2nd ed. Taylor & Francis, Abingdon, Oxon. 2004.

III.
- 7. **B**
- 8. **B, D**
- 9. **C, D, E, F**
- 10. **B, D**

IV.
- 11. **E**
- 12. **C**
- 13. **B**

V.
- 14. **D**
- 15. **A, B, E**
- 16. **C**

VI.
- 17. **B**
- 18. **C**
- 19. **A**
- 20. **D**
- 21. **A**
  Bymaster, F P, *et al.*: Fluoxetine, but not other selective serotonin uptake inhibitors, increases norepinephrine and dopamine extracellular levels in prefrontal cortex. *Psychopharmacology (Berl)* 160 (4): 353-361. 2002.

  Owens, J M, Knight, D L, Nemeroff, C B: Second generation SSRIS: human monoamine transporter binding profile of escitalopram and R-fluoxetine. *Encephale* 28(4): 350-355. 2002.

VII.
- 22. **C**
- 23. **G**
- 24. **D**
  Taylor, D, Paton, C & Kerwin, R: *The Maudsley Prescribing Guidelines*, 9th ed. Informa Healthcare, London. 2007.

VIII.
>   **25.** A, E
>   **26.** A, D, F
>   **27.** A, C

IX.
>   **28.** B
>   **29.** A
>   **30.** F

X.
>   **31.** B, E
>   **32.** B, G
>   **33.** B, D

XI.
>   **34.** B, D
>   **35.** C, E
>   **36.** A, F

XII.
>   **37.** C, F
>   **38.** A, D
>   **39.** B, E

XIII.
>   **40.** B
>   **41.** E
>   **42.** C

XIV.
>   **43.** B
>   **44.** A
>   **45.** C

XV.
>   **46.** B
>   **47.** C
>   **48.** A

XVI.
>   **49.** H
>   **50.** A
>   **51.** A, B, E
>   **52.** C, G

>   Serotonin is derived from tryptophan by a two-step enzymatic process. Tryptophan is first converted to 5-hydroxytryptophan by tryptophan hydroxylase and then to serotonin by L aromatic acid decarboxylase. This

enzyme also decarboxylates DOPA, the catechol amino acid formed from tyrosine, to dopamine in the first step of monoamine catechol neurotransmitter biosynthesis. Catechol neurotransmitter biosynthesis is initiated by tyrosine hydroxylase which hydroxylates tyrosine to form DOPA. Noradrenalin and adrenaline are synthesized from dopamine by sequential hydroxylation and methylation reactions. Dopamine β-hydroxylase converts dopamine into noradrenalin, which is then methylated by phenyl ethanolamine N-methyl transferase to form adrenaline.

Hyland, K: Neurochemistry and defects of biogenic amine neurotransmitter metabolism. *J Inherit Metab Dis* 22, 353-363. 1999.

XVII.
  53. A, B
  54. A, B
  55. B
  56. A, E
  57. A, B
    The D_1 and D_5 receptors are members of the D_1-like family of dopamine receptors, whereas the D_2, D_3 and D_4 receptors are members of the D_2-like family. All dopamine receptors are coupled to G proteins. D_1-like family receptors increase cAMP whereas D_2-like family receptors decrease cAMP and/or increase IP3.

    Girault & Greengard: The neurobiology of dopamine signaling. *Arch Neurol* 61 (5): 641–644. 2004.

XVIII.
  58. F
    Cerebellopontine angle tumours include vestibular schwannoma (i.e. acoustic neuroma) as well as infratentorial ependymoma, brainstem glioma, medulloblastoma, or neurofibromatosis.
  59. A
  60. G
  61. C
    Neurological signs and symptoms, such as nystagmus, that do not lessen when the patient focuses, point to central causes of vertigo. Cerebrovascular disease, tumours, migraine and multiple sclerosis are leading causes of central vertigo. Vertigo is also associated with various mood states, anxiety, personality and substance

misuse disorders.

Labuguen, R: Initial Evaluation of Vertigo. *Am Fam Physician* 73: 244-251, 254. 2006.

XIX.

62. A, C, G
PET scan can also quantify receptor functions depending on isotope used.

63. E, H, J
One of the most robust features of the Evoked Potential or Event-Related Potential (ERP) response is a response to unpredictable stimuli. This response is known as the P300 or P3 response as it manifests as a positive deflection in voltage approximately 300 milliseconds after the stimulus is presented.

Luck, S: *An Introduction to the Event-related Potential Technique*. MIT Press. 2005.

64. C, F
fMRI has poor temporal resolution and measures neuronal activity indirectly.

65. B, D
EEG has poor spatial resolution of up to several centimetres as compared to 2 to 3 millimetres for fMRI.

Krakow, K, *et al.*: EEG recording during fMRI experiments: image quality. *Hum Brain Mapp* 10, 10± 15. 2000.

XX.

66. A, F
67. E
68. C
69. F

XXI.

70. F
71. A
72. B

XXII.

73. G
74. E
75. G

XXIII.

76. F
77. E

78. K
XXIV.
  79. B
  80. H
  81. E
XXV.
  82. G
  83. C
  84. A
XXVI.
  85. E
  86. D
  87. B
  88. B
XXVII.
  89. C, E, H
  90. B, D, F, I
  91. A, G
XXVIII.
  92. B, D, E, I
  93. B, C, F, G
XXIX.
  94. C, D
  95. A
  96. A
  97. E, H
XXX.
  98. G
  99. C
  100. E
XXXI.
  101. A, G
  102. C
  103. I
XXXII.
  104. H
  105. D, E
  106. F, G
  107. A, B, C
XXXIII.
  108. C
  109. A

110. B
XXXIV.
   111. H
   112. B
   113. E
XXXV.
   114. F
   115. B
   116. E
XXXVI.
   117. D
   118. A
   119. C
XXXVII.
   120. E
   121. B
   122. H
XXXVIII.
   123. C
   124. B
   125. D
XXXIX.
   126. D
   127. C
   128. A
XL.
   129. C
   130. E
   131. B
XLI.
   132. B
   133. D
   134. A

XLII.
   135. B
   136. E
   137. A
XLIII.
   138. G
   139. C
   140. A

141. D
142. F
Semple, D, *et al.*: *Oxford Handbook of Psychiatry*. 2005.

XLIV.
143. E, I – Wilson's disease
144. A, F – Huntington's disease
145. B, J – Cri-du Chat syndrome

XLV.
146. D
147. G
148. A
149. F

XLVI.
150. E
151. A
152. B
153. C
154. D

XLVII.
155. D, I
156. A, F
157. B, H

Chapter 15a – Mock examination

Instructions
You have 3 hours to complete the exam. The maximum score is 200.
Each answer has one mark. Please note that each component of EMI
has one mark. It is advised that the paper is attempted under exam
conditions and should be completed in one sitting.
Good luck!

---

1. Cohort studies:

A. Cannot study rare exposures
B. Are suitable for rare outcomes
C. Are usually quick to perform
D. Are suitable for randomisation
E. Can assess multiple outcomes

2. Randomised Control Trials:

A. Cannot be meta-analysed
B. Measure effectiveness
C. Minimise selection bias
D. Are less time consuming
E. Cannot measure efficacy

3. Cross-over RCT is a type of RCT classified according to:

A. The unit of analysis
B. How the participants are exposed to the interventions
C. The number of participants
D. The different aspects of the interventions they evaluate
E. Whether the investigators and participants know which
   intervention is being assessed

4. Pragmatic trials:

A. Are not reflective of every-day practice
B. Measure efficacy
C. Have less dropout rate
D. Measure effectiveness
E. Tend to use more restrictive inclusion criteria

5. The following statements about systematic reviews are true, except:

A. Systematic reviews may suffer from publication bias
B. Systematic reviews require the formulation of a specific question
C. Systematic reviews may suffer from location bias
D. Systematic reviews require pre-specification of inclusion and exclusion criteria for articles
E. Systematic reviews require statistical meta-analysis

6. In an economic analysis, if the important outcome is multidimensional, then the most appropriate method of analysis would be:

A. Cost minimisation analysis
B. Cost effectiveness analysis
C. Cost utility analysis
D. Cost benefit analysis
E. Cost consequences analysis

7. Which of the following studies is an analytical observational study?

A. Survey
B. Case report
C. Case series
D. Cohort study
E. Qualitative study

8. Descriptive observational studies:

A. Can distinguish between cause and effect
B. Are not vulnerable to bias
C. Generally have a control group for comparison
D. Are suitable for hypothesis generation
E. Are suitable for hypothesis testing

9. Which one of the following is an experimental study?

A. RCT
B. Cross-sectional survey
C. Cohort study
D. Qualitative study
E. Case series

10. A study is being designed to compare an established treatment for depression with a new treatment. Patients are allocated to different groups by using their date of birth. Patients with their date of birth starting with an odd number are allocated to the new treatment group and the ones with an even number are allocated to the established treatment group. What study design is this?

A. Open trial
B. Randomised control trial
C. Quasi-randomised control trial
D. Cross-over trial
E. Pragmatic trial

11. Types of selection bias include the following, except:

A. Berkson bias
B. Diagnostic purity bias
C. Membership bias
D. Interviewer bias
E. Historical control bias

12. Types of observation bias include the following, except:

A. Interviewer bias
B. Recall bias
C. Neyman bias
D. Hawthorne effect
E. Obsequiousness bias

13. The most reliable way to avoid selection bias is:

A. By using inclusion criteria
B. By using exclusion criteria
C. By matching
D. By randomisation
E. By limiting the sample size

14. The following methods can reduce confounding, except:

A. Restriction
B. Matching
C. Per-protocol analysis
D. Randomisation
E. Stratification

15. A study is designed to look at the aetiology of anorexia nervosa. All the patients with diagnosis of anorexia nervosa are selected from the database of a psychiatric hospital. A control group matched for age and sex, without the diagnosis of anorexia nervosa, is used for comparison. All the case notes are then studied to identify factors during childhood which could be associated with the development of anorexia nervosa in later life. The study design is:

A. Cohort study
B. Case-control study
C. Ecological study
D. Controlled trial
E. Pragmatic trial

16. You want to assess a new drug for insomnia. You decide to give this drug to all your patients suffering from insomnia. The effects and side effects are explained to the patients prior to administration and the response is observed over the next 2 weeks. The above study design is:

A. Quasi-randomised trial
B. Open trial
C. Cluster trial
D. Pragmatic trial
E. Randomised control trial

17. In order to assess a new treatment for schizophrenia, you divide all your patients with schizophrenia into two groups. One group is given quetiapine and the other group is given the new treatment. The response is compared over the next 6 months. The study design used here is:

A. Open trial
B. Controlled trial
C. Quasi-randomised trial
D. Cross-over trial
E. Factorial design RCT

18. When comparing more than two groups, the most appropriate parametric test would be:

A. Median
B. Man-Whitney U test
C. Friedman test
D. Chi-squared test
E. ANOVA

19. The Likelihood Ratio for Negative Test can be calculated by using the following formula:

A. (1 – Sensitivity)/Specificity
B. Sensitivity/(1 – Specificity)
C. a/(a + b)
D. d/(c + d)
E. a/(a + c)

20. The most appropriate statistical test to determine whether a personas sex, weight and cholesterol level affect their blood glucose level would be:

A. Paired t test
B. Chi-squared test
C. Regression
D. Multiple regression
E. McNemar's test

21. Recent research findings suggest DOA as a susceptibility locus for which of the following disorders?

A. Schizophrenia
B. Bipolar affective disorder
C. ADHD
D. Psychopathic traits
E. Generalised anxiety disorder

22. Patients with velocardiofacial syndrome are at significant risk of developing psychiatric disorders. The risk of these patients of developing schizophrenia is:

A. 1 in 2
B. 1 in 4
C. 1 in 6
D. 1 in 10

E.   1 in 12

23. The most common inherited cause of learning disability is:

A.   Turner's syndrome
B.   Klinefelter's syndrome
C.   Down's syndrome
D.   Fragile X syndrome
E.   Aicardi syndrome

24. Deletion of the distal short arm of chromosome 4 is known to cause:

A.   Cri-du Chat syndrome
B.   Wolf-Hirschhorn syndrome
C.   Williams syndrome
D.   Prader-Willi syndrome
E.   Tuberose Sclerosis II

25. Chromosome 7q has been associated with which of the following disorders?

A.   Wolf-Hirschhorn
B.   Wilson's Disease
C.   ASD
D.   Neurofibromatosis
E.   DiGeorge syndrome

26. Which one of the following disorders has been found to have significant linkage and association with the region 1q41?

A.   Bipolar affective disorder
B.   Schizophrenia
C.   Obsessive compulsive disorder
D.   Generalised anxiety disorder
E.   Depression

27. Linkage analysis suggests an association between the serotonin transporter gene (17q11.1-12) and the following disease:

A.   Bipolar affective disorder
B.   Schizophrenia

C. Depression
D. Obsessive compulsive disorder
E. Anorexia nervosa

28. Mutation in the MCEP2 gene causes which of the following disorders?

A. Tuberous sclerosis
B. Rett syndrome
C. Neurofibromatosis
D. Williams syndrome
E. Angelman syndrome

29. A 45-year-old patient suffering from Huntington's disease (HD) attends your clinic for the treatment of depression. He is accompanied by his 24-year-old daughter. The daughter asks you what are her chances of developing HD?

A. Zero % as she can only be a carrier
B. 20%
C. 30%
D. 50%
E. 60%

30. Most studies suggest the estimate of relative risk of unipolar depression in first-degree relatives of patients with unipolar depression to be in the range of:

A. 01-02
B. 1.5-03
C. 3.5-05
D. 03-05
E. 05-10

31. The gene for amyloid precursor protein on the long arm of chromosome 21 is strongly associated with which of the following disorders?

A. Dementia of Alzheimer's type
B. Lewy body dementia
C. Huntington's disease
D. CJD

E. Vascular dementia

32. A highly selective deficit in the recognition of disgust has been confirmed in those whom genetic testing proved to be gene carriers for which of the following diseases?

A. Schizophrenia
B. Huntington's
C. Alzheimer's
D. Parkinson's
E. Neurofibromatosis

33. Which of the following syndromes is X-linked recessive?

A. Fragile X syndrome
B. Lesch-Nyhan syndrome
C. Trisomy X
D. Neurofibromatosis
E. Laurence-Moon syndrome

34. Lifetime risk of unipolar depression in a monozygotic twin is:

A. 20-30%
B. 30-50%
C. 50-60%
D. 60-70%
E. 70-80%

35. Molecular genetics research shows some support for the implication of RGS4 in the aetiology of:

A. PTSD
B. Depression
C. Bipolar affective disorder
D. Schizophrenia
E. Bulimia nervosa

36. Which of the following diseases is autosomal recessive?

A. Sturge-Weber syndrome
B. Hurler syndrome
C. Tuberous sclerosis

D. Von Hippel-Lindau syndrome
E. Neurofibromatosis

37. Mutation in the CREBBP gene causes which one of the following disorders?

A. Smith-Magenis syndrome
B. Miller-Dieker syndrome
C. Wolf-Hirschhorn syndrome
D. Williams syndrome
E. Rubinstein Tyabi syndrome

38. The RELN gene is considered to be an important contributor to genetic risk in:
A. Conduct disorder
B. ADHD
C. Autism
D. OCD
E. Oppositional defiant disorder

39. The risk of having alcohol problems in first-degree relatives of alcoholics is:

A. 2 times
B. 3 times
C. 4 times
D. 5 times
E. 6 times

40. The most common genetic cause of learning disability is:

A. Turner's syndrome
B. Klinefelter's syndrome
C. Down's syndrome
D. Trisomy X
E. Aicardi syndrome

41. Which one of the following connections for septum is an efferent connection?

A. Cingulate gyrus
B. Stria medullaris

C. Brainstem
D. Olfactory tract
E. Amygdala

42. Which one of the following structures promotes sleep?

A. Raphe nuclei
B. Nucleus coeruleus
C. Tuberomammillary nucleus
D. Midbrain cholinergic nuclei
E. Ventrolateral preoptic nucleus

43. Which one of the following statements is true for dreams?

A. They are more easily recalled in NREM sleep
B. Factors such as salience and arousal have no role in dream recall
C. Brain activity is higher in frontal lobes than in limbic system during dreams
D. In lucid dreaming a person is in control of the characters and the environment of the dream
E. Contents of dreams are less emotional than similar real-life events

44. Which one of the following is true for stages of sleep?

A. K complexes are present in stage 2
B. It takes about 4 hours to descend through stages 1–4
C. REM sleep lasts for about one hour after stages 1–4
D. Muscle tone is very low during stages 1–4
E. There are two cycles per average sleep period

45. Which one of the following is more suggestive of a pseudoseizure than a seizure?

A. Related to sleep deprivation
B. Sudden onset and termination
C. Patient sustains injuries
D. Reflexes impaired
E. Normal prolactin levels at 15 minutes post-seizure

46. Which one of the following is true for depression Parkinson's disease?

A. It is related to the severity of the disease
B. Excessive guilt is present
C. Suicide is common
D. It is associated with dementia
E. It usually occurs after the onset of motor symptoms

47. Which one of the following is true for Pick's disease?

A. Late loss of executive functions
B. Lexical anomia
C. Frontotemporal hypometabolism
D. Fluent aphasia
E. Personality is preserved

48. Which one of the following is true for suggestive features of Lewy body dementia?

A. REM sleep behaviour disorder
B. Mild neuroleptic sensitivity
C. High dopamine transporter uptake in basal ganglia on functional neuroimaging
D. High occipital activity on functional neuroimaging
E. Severe damage to medial temporal lobe on structural neuroimaging

49. Which one of the following is true for Wilson's disease?

A. Autosomal dominant disease
B. Patient gets symptomatic by age 20–30 years
C. Psychiatric symptoms correlate with liver disease
D. Copper is accumulated in prefrontal cortex
E. Males are affected more frequently

50. Which one of the following is true for Fahr's disease?

A. Autosomal recessive disease
B. Presents in third to fifth decade
C. Bilateral calcification of hippocampus
D. Clear correlation between age of onset and extent of calcification
E. Premorbid psychomotor development is delayed

51. Which one of the following is true for Huntington's disease?

A. Autosomal recessive disease
B. Somatostatin levels are decreased
C. GABA levels in the striatum are increased
D. Suicide is among the leading causes of death about 14 years after the diagnosis
E. Substance misuse is more common than in general population

52. Which one of the following is a good prognostic factor for recovery from traumatic brain injury?

A. Increased age
B. Chronic substance abuse
C. Preserved olfaction
D. Past psychiatric history
E. Learning disability

53. Which one of the following is true for AIDS dementia?

A. Neurons are directly targeted by HIV
B. Atrophy of brain is evident by widened sulci
C. Basal ganglia is indirectly affected
D. gp120 protein reversibly binds to calcium channels
E. ventricular size is increased

54. Which one of the following is true for psychiatric problems in patients with AIDS dementia?

A. Delirium is common
B. More than half have depression
C. About a third have suicidal ideation
D. Mania is not reported
E. Prior history of depression is a protective factor

55. Which one of the following is true for psychiatric problems in patients with SLE?

A. Psychiatric symptoms once developed are permanent
B. Cognitive impairment once developed continues to get worse gradually
C. Short-term memory loss is not associated with systemic disease activity

D. Suicidality is increased in active disease and is associated with fast EEG rhythm
E. Up to 75% of patients may have neuropsychiatric problems

56. Which one of the following statements is true for Creutzfeldt-Jakob disease?

A. Slow progressive dementia
B. Myoclonus occurs rarely
C. Biphasic spikes on EEG
D. Diffusion Weighted Imaging is most sensitive
E. 14-3-3 protein is reduced in CSF

57. Which one of the following is true for Friedreich's ataxia?

A. It is the most common of the inherited ataxia
B. Autosomal dominant neurodegenerative disease
C. Cognitive decline is the first symptom
D. Personality is preserved
E. Hypertonicity

58. Which one of the following is not a risk factor for depression in Parkinson's disease?

A. Greater degree of left brain involvement
B. History of depression
C. Ataxia
D. Bradykinesis
E. Male gender

59. Which one of the following statements is true for Gilles de la Tourette's syndrome?

A. Average age of onset is 18 years
B. Multiple phonic tics with one or two motor tics
C. Strong association with OCD and ADHD
D. Coprolalia is required to be present to make a diagnosis
E. Common in females

60. Which one of the following statements is true for Gelineau's syndrome?
A. Insomnia is a main feature

B. Blurred vision is a recognised symptom
C. Common in females
D. Generally first symptoms occur after 50 years of age
E. Auditory hallucinations are more common than visual hallucinations

61. Which one of the following is a feature of NREM sleep?

A. Decreased parasympathetic activity
B. Upward ocular deviation
C. Increased cerebral blood flow
D. Penile erection/increased vaginal blood flow
E. Maximal loss of muscle tone

62. Which one of the following syndromes is caused by full-blown bilateral occipital damage?

A. Aicardi syndrome
B. Dandy Walker syndrome
C. Williams syndrome
D. Balint's syndrome
E. Duane's syndrome

63. Which one of the following statements is true for aggression in seizures?

A. It is common
B. It is associated with depression
C. It is typically co-ordinated and directed
D. It is positively correlated with severity of seizure
E. It is associated with post-ictal paranoid psychosis

64. Which one of the following is true for psychiatric presentations of brain tumours?

A. Right-sided tumours present with euphoria
B. Delusions caused by tumours are typically complex
C. Auditory hallucinations are more frequent than visual
D. Left-sided tumours present with underestimation of seriousness of illness
E. Right-sided tumours are associated with akinesia

65. Which one of the following psychiatric symptoms tends to present with slow-growing brain tumours?

A. Cognitive dysfunction
B. Psychosis
C. Vague personality changes
D. Severe agitation
E. Mania

66. Which one of the following is true for a comparison between Variant Creutzfeldt-Jakob disease (vCJD) and Creutzfeldt-Jakob disease (CJD)?

A. vCJD affects younger patients
B. vCJD has a shorter duration of illness
C. Psychiatric symptoms in vCJD are not prominent
D. Dementia and myoclonus occur early in vCJD
E. vCJD has diagnostic EEG abnormalities

67. Which one of the following is a characteristic of temperament?

A. Compassion
B. Coldness
C. Iniquity
D. Prejudice
E. Intensity of reaction

68. Which one of the following characteristics is present in an infant with a slow to warm up temperament?

A. Irritable
B. Playful
C. Relatively inactive
D. Responds intensely and negatively to new situations
E. Adapts readily to new situations

69. Which one of the following statements is true with regards to scores on various indices by families of school-refusing children?

A. High score on child independence
B. Low score on participation in recreational activity
C. Low score in hostility

D. Low score in conflict
E. Low score in protection

70. Which one of the following statements is true for attachment in infants?

A. Attachment behaviours start to occur at about the age of 6 months and decrease by 3 years
B. Securely attached don't need to interact with the mother during a reunion episode
C. Insecurely attached seek interaction with the mother during a reunion episode
D. Ambivalent infants show contradictory behaviours to the mother during a reunion episode
E. Disorganised infants show resistance to the mother during a reunion episode

71. Which one of the following statements is true with regards to the effects of family structure on the psychosocial development of a child?

A. Two lesbian parents may lead to emotional problems
B. Single parent is not associated with any harmful effect
C. Extended families involvement may lead to behavioural problems
D. Large family size may lead to educational problems
E. Oldest child has a slight disadvantage in intellectual development

72. Which one of the following statements is true with regards to the effects of various parenting styles?

A. Authoritative style is associated with an increased psychopathology rate
B. Permissive parenting generally leads to immature individuals
C. Authoritarian style promotes independence
D. Authoritative parents typically punish instead of forgiving
E. Children with permissive parents are happy and have good self-control

73. Which one of the following statements is true for families of children and adolescents with ADHD?

A. Higher rates of authoritative parenting
B. Low levels of parental negativity
C. Higher rates of ADHD in adopted children
D. Lower rates of authoritarian parenting
E. Mothers are more negative towards their daughters

74. Which one of the following is not a vulnerability factor for depression in women described by Brown and Harris?

A. Early maternal loss
B. Unemployment
C. Lack of a confiding relationship
D. Three or more children under the age of 14 at home
E. Family history of depression

75. Which one of the following is true for anterograde amnesia?

A. Priming is always spared
B. Priming is affected with medial temporal lobe lesions
C. Priming is affected with damage to occipital circuitry
D. Hippocampal damage is primarily associated with recognition memory deficits
E. Memories based on recollection are less severely affected as compared to the memories based on familiarity judgements

76. Which one of the following statements is true for retrograde amnesia?

A. It is frequently temporally graded
B. Flat retrograde amnesia is more common
C. Anterograde and retrograde amnesia cannot occur in the same patient
D. It has a genetic predisposition
E. According to Ribot's Law recent memories are more easily accessible

77. Which one of the following statements is true for dysfluent expressive dysphasia?

A. Damage is to the arcuate fasciculus
B. Speech is normal
C. Comprehension is lost

D. Person is unable to repeat what is said to him
E. Broca's area is affected

78. Which one of the following statements is true with regards to improving memory?

A. The key word method is very helpful in learning the vocabulary of foreign language
B. Capacity of working memory can be increased
C. Long-term memory is increased by chunking
D. Method of loci uses chunking to improve memory
E. Elaboration while encoding has no effect on later retrieval

79. Which one of the following tests is used to assess premorbid IQ?

A. Halstead Category test
B. Revised Wechsler Adult Intelligence scale
C. Seashore Rhythms test
D. National Adult Reading test
E. Complex Figure of Rey test

80. Which one of the following is true for means and standard deviations of Wechsler's Intelligence scales?

A. Means are 120 and standard deviations are 20
B. Means are 110 and standard deviations are 10
C. Means are 100 and standard deviations are 15
D. Means are 90 and standard deviations are 10
E. Means are 80 and standard deviations are 20

81. Which one of the following is not used as leverage for treatment adherence in mentally ill patients?

A. Money
B. Housing
C. Covert methods
D. Criminal justice
E. Outpatient commitment

82. Which one of the following statements is true for Eye Movement Desensitisation and Reprocessing?

A. It is carried out in 10 phases
B. It stimulates the dominant side of the brain
C. In instillation phase therapist asks the patient about negative cognitions
D. During the processing phase the patient focuses on a disturbing memory for 5 minutes
E. The desensitisation phase ends when subjective units of disturbance scale reaches 0 or 1

83. Which one of the following has the best evidence in treatment for bulimia nervosa?

A. Self-help manuals
B. IPT
C. Psychodynamic psychotherapy
D. CAT
E. CBT

84. Which one of the following statements is not true for post-traumatic amnesia?

A. It is a poor indicator of the extent of cognitive damage after a traumatic brain injury
B. If its duration is less than 24 hours with a GCS of above 12, the injury is categorised as mild
C. If its duration is between 1 and 7 days with a GCS of 9–11, the injury is categorised as moderate
D. If its duration is between 1 and 4 weeks with a GCS of 3–8, the injury is categorised as severe
E. If its duration is more than 4 weeks, the injury is categorised as very severe

85. Which one of the following is not a recognised risk factor for dementia in Parkinson's disease?

A. Older age
B. Early onset Parkinson's disease
C. Low socioeconomic status and education
D. Greater severity of extra-pyramidal symptoms
E. Susceptibility to psychosis with L-dopa

86. Which one of the following statements is incorrect for psychosis

in Parkinson's disease?
A. Presentation may be early or late in the course of Parkinson's disease
B. Auditory hallucinations are the most frequent psychotic phenomena
C. Increasing age is a risk factor
D. Therapy with multiple drugs is a risk factor
E. Cognitive impairment is a risk factor

87. Which one of the following statements is not true regarding Flumazenil?

A. It is a benzodiazepine (BZP) receptor agonist
B. It can be given through intramuscular route
C. It can reverse acute toxic effects of BZP
D. It carries a risk of provoking BZP withdrawals
E. It produces little pharmacological effect itself

88. The half-life of Chlordiazepoxide is:

A. 2-6 hours
B. 5-11 hours
C. 5-30 hours
D. 6-8 hours
E. 20-100 hours

89. Which one of the following drugs does not belong to Selective Serotonin Reuptake Inhibitor (SSRI)?

A. Fluoxetine
B. Paroxetine
C. Venlafaxine
D. Fluvoxamine
E. Escitalopram

90. One of the following statements is not true regarding Amisulpride:

A. It selectively blocks pre-synaptic dopamine receptors, at lower doses
B. At higher doses, it is relatively selective for striatal areas
C. It has low potential for extra-pyramidal side effects (EPSE)

D. It is a potent elevator of serum prolactin level
E. It is relatively free from anti-cholinergic side-effects

91. Which one of the following statements is not true for Paliperidone:

A. It is a major metabolite of quetiapine
B. Has low potential for EPSE
C. Is a D2 and 5HT2a antagonist
D. Is formulated as an osmotic release oral delivery system (OROS)
E. Doses between 6-12mg are more effective than placebo

92. Which one of the following is not true regarding the pharmacokinetics of psychotropic drugs?

A. Most psychotropic drugs are lipophilic
B. Most are largely bound to plasma proteins
C. Tend to have large volume of distribution
D. Excretion is mainly through bile
E. Large oral doses required due to first pass metabolism

93. All of the following statements are true for pharmacogenetics, except:

A. Mutations in the gene for CYP2D6 may be associated with antipsychotic drug-induced tardive dyskinesia
B. Weight gain with antipsychotic drugs is associated with an allele of the 5-HT1c receptor
C. Alleles associated with decreased expression of 5-HT transporter are associated with poorer response to SSRIs
D. Polymorphic variation in DNA may result in the production of the proteins that interact in different ways with psychotropic drugs
E. Therapeutic response to clozapine may be associated with specific alleles of the 5-HT2a receptor

94. All of the following statements are true for St John's Wort (SJW), except:

A. It is effective in the treatment of mild to moderate depression
B. It is an enzyme inducer
C. It is the popular name for the plant *Hypericum perforatum*
D. It can reduce the plasma concentration of the oral contraceptive

pill and can lead to treatment failure
E. It is associated with photosensitivity reactions

95. Adverse effects of monoamine oxidase inhibitors (MAOIs) include all of the following, except:

A. Weight gain
B. Sexual dysfunction
C. Peripheral neuropathy
D. Leucocytosis
E. Hypertensive crisis

96. Which one of the following drugs does not have any effect on Qt interval?

A. Methadone
B. Haloperidol
C. Intravenous administration of any antipsychotic
D. Mirtazapine
E. Pimozide

97. All of the following statements are true for lithium, except:

A. It is rapidly absorbed from GIT but has a long distribution phase
B. Plasma level can be expected to fall by 0.4mmol/l between 12 and 24 hours post-dose
C. It takes approximately 7 days to achieve a steady serum level
D. Aim is to keep plasma level between 0.6 to 1.0mmol/l
E. Children and adolescents may require higher serum level than adults

98. All of the following statements are true for bupropion, except:

A. It is licensed as an adjunct to smoking withdrawal in UK
B. Its antidepressant effect is equivalent to SSRIs
C. It causes sexual dysfunction
D. It is associated with increased risk of seizures
E. It should not be used in patients with history of eating disorder

99. Which one of the following antidepressants is not a MAOI?

A. Phenelzine

B. Tranylcypromine
C. Isocarboxazid
D. Moclobemide
E. Mianserin

100. Characteristic features of Neuroleptic Malignant syndrome (NMS) include all of the following, except:

A. Fluctuating level of consciousness
B. Tachycardia
C. Leucopoenia
D. Muscular rigidity
E. Hyperthermia

101. All of the following antipsychotic drugs are correctly paired with male sexual dysfunction, except:

A. Haloperidol: decreased ejaculation
B. Chlorpromazine: reduced libido and impotence
C. Mesoridazine: anejaculation
D. Flufenazine: decreased libido
E. Trifluperazine: impaired ejaculation

102. Which one of the following statements is false about SSRIs?

A. Each SSRI produces approximately a 60% overall response rate
B. Paroxetine, fluoxetine, and sertraline are similar in effectiveness for major depression and depression with high levels of anxiety
C. Patients who discontinue one SSRI for lack of tolerability or response can be effectively treated with another
D. Paroxetine has a slower onset of antidepressants effect than other SSRIs
E. Sertraline has advantages over paroxetine in the treatment of panic disorder

103. Trazadone can be used as 'off label' in all of the following conditions, except:

A. Diabetic nephropathy
B. Bulimia nervosa
C. Alcohol withdrawal
D. Erectile dysfunction
E. Fibromyalgia

104. All of the following statements are true for pharmacokinetic properties of depot antipsychotic drugs, except:

A. Haloperidol decanoate requires 3-9 days to reach peak plasma level
B. Risperidone slow-release injection requires 28 days to reach peak plasma level
C. Pipothiazine palmitate requires 4 weeks to reach steady state
D. Fluphenazine decanoate requires 1-2 days to reach peak plasma level
E. Flupenthixol decanoate is usually administered every two weeks

105. All of the following statements are correct, except:

A. Maclobemide should not be combined with venlafaxine
B. Mirtazapine has major inhibitory effects on cytochrome P450 isoenzymes
C. Trazodone is a triazolopyridine derivative
D. Duloxetine is classified as a selective serotonin and noradrenaline reuptake inhibitor (SNRI)
E. Hypericum extracts may induce hepatic enzymes

106. All of the following statements are correct regarding antipsychotic drugs, except:

A. D2 receptor occupancy is 80% for haloperidol
B. They are contraindicated in Addison's disease and glaucoma
C. D2 receptor occupancy is 75% for clozapine
D. Chlorpromazine has been associated with cholestatic jaundice
E. Pimozide has been associated with serious cardiac arrhythmias

107. Which one of the following statements is not true according to the survey of mental health of children and adolescents in England and Wales?

A. The proportion of children and adolescents with any mental disorder was greater among boys than girls
B. The proportions of children with any mental disorder were 13% for boys and 10% for girls
C. 10% of white children and 12% of black children were assessed as having a mental health problem
D. Children of lone parents were about four times as likely to

have a mental health problem than those living with married or cohabiting couples

E. Families with two children had the lowest rate of mental disorder compared with those who were part of four- and five-children households

108. The survey of the mental health of young people looked after by local authorities in England (2002) showed the following characteristics, except:

A. The survey focused on the prevalence of mental health problems among young people aged 5–17
B. 45% were assessed as having a mental disorder
C. 5- to 10-year-olds, those looked after by local authorities, were about five times more likely to have a mental disorder
D. 70% presented with conduct disorder
E. The rates of emotional disorders were similar for boys and girls

109. The percentage of adults with borderline intelligence, according to the UK-wide cross-sectional survey on psychiatric morbidity and social functioning among adults living in private households, is:

A. 2.3%
B. 5.3%
C. 8.3%
D. 12.3%
E. 15.3%

110. Which one of the following statements is not true with regards to Schizotypal Personality Questionnaire (SPQ)?

A. It can be used with both adults and adolescents
B. It has a brief version (SPQ-B) with 30 items
C. It measures three factors of schizotypy: cognitive-perceptual, interpersonal, and disorganised
D. It has a total of 74 items
E. It was developed by Adrian Raine

111. Which one of the following statements is not true with regards to the Positive and Negative Syndrome Scale (PANSS)?

A. It is widely used in psychiatric research

B. It is administered by the clinician
C. It is a 30-item scale with 16 general psychopathology symptom items
D. It has eight positive-symptom items, and eight negative-symptom items
E. It may have possible scores from 30 to 210

112. The cross-sectional surveys are useful for all of the following, except:

A. Planning services and identifying needs both met and unmet
B. Charting trends over time
C. Diagnosing disorders like schizophrenia
D. Drawing political attention to the extent of a problem within a community
E. Making comparisons with other populations and regions

113. The following statements are true regarding epidemiology of depressive disorder, except:

A. Prevalence is 5-10% in primary care settings
B. It will be the second leading cause of disability and morbidity by 2020
C. 75% of the deaths are due to suicide in persons aged 20-35 years
D. Mortality rate may be as high as 15% in persons with mood disorders
E. Prevalence of depressive symptoms may be 30% in patients presenting to their GPs

114. All of the following are true about delusional disorder, except:

A. Erotomania is more common in women
B. 80% are married
C. It may account for 5% of psychiatric admissions
D. Prevalence is estimated at 0.025-0.03
E. Delusional jealousy is more common in men

115. The following statements are not true about schizotypal disorder, except:

A. Approximately 3% of the general population may be associated
B. 10% of psychiatric admissions are associated with it
C. RCTs support use of olanzapine to treat it

D. The disorder tends to run a very unstable course
E. It is classified along with cluster A/odd eccentric personality disorders in ICD-10

116. All of the following are true about Parkinson's disease, except:

A. 25% of the patients are disabled or die in 5 years
B. It typically presents after 70 years of age
C. 5% of cases are familial
D. Male to female ratio is 3:2
E. 20-30% of the patients may show some cognitive decline

117. Which one of the following statements is not true about HIV/AIDS?

A. 70-80% may develop cognitive disorder
B. There is 50 x increased risk of suicide in those infected with the virus
C. 30% patients may present with delirium
D. 30-50% of the patients may show depressive symptoms after the diagnosis
E. 30% develop HIV-associated dementia (HAD)

118. Which one of the following authors published *Three Essays on the Theory of Sexuality*?

A. Jung
B. Freud
C. Klein
D. Erickson
E. Berne

119. Transactional analysis is associated with:

A. Berne
B. Jung
C. Freud
D. Winnicott
E. Klein

120. The number of distinct forms of psychotherapy identified is:

A. 5
B. 10
C. 50
D. 100
E. Over 450

121. Which one of the following is not one of the five principal kinds of psychotherapy?

A. Psychodynamic
B. Cognitive behavioural
C. Integrative
D. Cognitive analytic therapy
E. Counselling

122. Which one of the following statements about dream works is not true?

A. It is a process of symbolisation
B. It is a process of elaboration
C. Can be consciously unravelled by the patient with the help of therapist
D. Helps converting manifest dream into latent dream
E. Is an essential part of examination of dreams

123. Which one of the following is a core feature of borderline personality disorder?

A. Attempts to avoid abandonment
B. Impulsivity
C. Poor self-esteem
D. Empty feeling
E. Self harm

EMIs

124–130 – Use of questionnaires in psychiatric disorders

Options

    A. Self-rated instrument
    B. Clinician-administered instrument

C. 9-items version
D. 10-items version
E. 14-items version
F. 24-items version
G. 30-items version
H. 45-items version
I. 60 items version

Lead in: For each of the following questionnaires, choose the most appropriate options from above.

Each option might be used once, more than once, or not at all.

i.   Patient Health Questionnaire-9 (PHQ-9) (choose <u>two</u> options)
ii.   General Health Questionnaire (GHQ) (choose <u>three</u> options)
iii. Geriatric Depression Scale (GDS) (choose <u>two</u> options)

131-134 – *Lesion localisation*

Options

A. Left frontal lobe lesion
B. Left parietal lobe lesion
C. Right parietal lobe lesion
D. Left temporal lobe lesion
E. Occipital lobe lesion
F. Bilateral occipito-parietal lesion

Lead in: Which of the above lesions are implicated in each of the following symptoms?

Each option might be used once, more than once, or not at all.

i.   Automatism (choose <u>one</u> option)
ii.   Anton's syndrome (choose <u>one</u> option)
iii. Agraphia (choose <u>two</u> options)

135-138 – *Neuroimaging*

Options

A. Parkinson's disease
B. Fahr's disease
C. Normal pressure hydrocephalus
D. Delirium
E. AIDS dementia
F. SLE
G. Huntington's disease
H. Wilson's disease
I. Progressive supra nuclear palsy
J. Pick's disease
K. Alzheimer's dementia

Lead in: Which of the above diseases correlate to each of the following neuroimaging results?

Each option might be used once, more than once, or not at all.

i. Decreased uptake in striatum on PET scan (choose two options)
ii. Medial temporal lobe atrophy on CT and MRI scan (choose one option)
iii. Hypoperfusion in the frontal convexity and orbitofrontal cortex on SPECT (choose one option)

139-141 – *Neuroimaging*

Options

A. Parkinson's disease
B. Fahr's disease
C. Normal pressure hydrocephalus
D. Delirium
E. AIDS dementia
F. SLE
G. Huntington's disease
H. Wilson's disease
I. Progressive supra nuclear palsy
J. Pick's disease
K. Alzheimer's dementia

Lead in: Which of the above diseases correlate to each of the following neuroimaging results?

Each option might be used once, more than once, or not at all.

i.   Mineral deposits in the basal ganglia, periventricular white matter and dentate nuclei on CT and MRI scans (choose <u>one</u> option)
ii. Frontal hypometabolism on PET and bilateral frontal hypoperfusion on SPECT scans (choose <u>one</u> option)
iii. Reflux into ventricles and no flow into the superior sagittal sinus on cisternography (choose <u>one</u> option)

142-144 – Perception

Options

A. Finger agnosia
B. Anosogosia
C. Prosopagnosia
D. Astereognosia
E. Simultanagnosia
F. Agraphaesthesia
G. Autotopagnosia
H. Hemisomatognosis

Lead in: Which of the above agnosias are best described in each of the question belows?

Each option might be used once, more than once, or not at all.

i.   Person is unable to recognise an object by palpation (choose <u>one</u> option)
ii. Person is unable to recognise his individual fingers (choose <u>one</u> option)
iii. Patient is unable to identify numbers or letters traced on his palm with his eyes closed (choose <u>one</u> option)

145-149 – Memory

Options

A. Episodic memory loss
B. Fast forgetting on recall tasks
C. Ribot's Law
D. Impaired priming
E. Semantic memory
F. Functional and structural changes in hippocampus and prefrontal cortex
G. Executive problems
H. Loss of personal identity
I. Temporary dysfunction in limbic-hippocampal circuits

Lead in: Which of the above are best associated with the memory problems described in each of the questions below?

Each option might be used once, more than once, or not at all.

i. Memory problems associated with damage to medial temporal lobe and occipital circuitry (choose two options)
ii. Memory problems associated with depression (choose two options)
iii. Global psychogenic amnesia (choose one option)

150-162 – *Neuropsychological tests*

Options

A. Trail-making test
B. Benton verbal fluency test
C. Complex figure of Rey
D. Speech sound perception test
E. Halstead category test
F. Benton visual retention test
G. Left-right disorientation test
H. Block design
I. Revised Wechsler memory scale
J. Seashore rhythms test
K. Object assembly
L. Wisconsin card sorting test

Lead in: Which of the above neuropsychological tests are used to test the functions of brain regions mentioned in each of the questions below?

Each option might be used once, more than once, or not at all.

   i.   Frontal lobe (choose <u>four</u> options)
   ii. Parietal lobe (choose <u>four</u> options)
  iii. Temporal lobe (choose <u>five</u> options)

163–168 – *Genetic disorders and features*

Options:

   A. Chorea
   B. Cat-like cry
   C. Elfin features
   D. Pronounced speech impairment
   E. Kayser-Fleisher rings
   F. Dementia
   G. Bouts of uncontrollable laughter
   H. Fear (phobia) of loud noise
   I. Wing-beating tremor
   J. Moon face

Lead in: Choose associations from the above list for each of the following options.

Each option might be used once, more than once, or not at all.

   i.   Chromosome 15 (choose <u>two</u> options)
   ii. Micro-deletion of chromosome 7 (choose <u>two</u> options)
  iii. Trinucleotide repeat of CAG on chromosome 4 (choose <u>two</u> options)

169–173 – *Genetic syndromes*

Options:

   A. Down's syndrome
   B. Hunter syndrome
   C. Klinefelter's syndrome
   D. Patau syndrome
   E. Turner's syndrome
   F. Edwards syndrome

   G. Fragile X syndrome

Lead in: Choose appropriate associations from the above options for each of the following types of genetic anomaly.

Each option might be used once, more than once, or not at all.

   i.   Autosomal trisomy (choose <u>three</u> options)
   ii.   XXY (choose <u>one</u> option)
   iii. X0 (choose <u>one</u> option)

<u>174–176 – *Study design*</u>

Options

   A. Survey
   B. Audit
   C. Cohort study
   D. Randomised control trial
   E. Open trial
   F. Cluster trial
   G. Ecological study
   H. Qualitative study
   I.   Pragmatic trial
   J.   Cross-over trial

Lead in: Choose the most appropriate study design from the above list for each of the following studies.

Each option might be used once, more than once, or not at all.

   i.   By using the national database, the vaccination records of all the patients in Sweden suffering with autism are checked to look for any association between MMR and autism (choose <u>one</u> option)
   ii.   All the drug cards in an adult in-patients unit are checked for the prescribing of antipsychotics to see compliance with NICE guidelines (choose <u>one</u> option)
   iii. 50 patients receiving home treatment are interviewed to get their feedback regarding the service, to compare in-patient services with community services (choose <u>one</u> option)

177–179 – *Bias*

Options

- A. Berkson bias
- B. Attrition bias
- C. Performance bias
- D. Diagnostic purity bias
- E. Neyman bias
- F. Recall bias
- G. Hawthorne effect
- H. Ascertainment bias
- I. Membership bias
- J. Diagnostic suspicion bias

Lead in: For each of the following descriptions, choose the appropriate options from the above list.

Each option might be used once, more than once, or not at all.

- i. Participants in a study may alter their behaviour if they are aware that they are being observed in a study (choose <u>one</u> option)
- ii. Systematic differences in the care provided to the participants in the comparison groups other than the intervention under investigation (choose <u>one</u> option)
- iii. Bias which is also called admission bias and arises when sample population is taken from a hospital setting (choose <u>one</u> option)

180–187 – *Statistical tests*

Options

- A. Mean
- B. Median
- C. Standard deviation
- D. Student's t test
- E. ANOVA
- F. Mann-Whitney U test
- G. Inter-quartile range
- H. Wilcoxon's rank sum test

I.   Kruskal-Wallis ANOVA
J.   Chi-squared test

Lead in: For each of the following, choose the most appropriate options from the above list.

Each option might be used once, more than once, or not at all.

i.   Parametric tests to describe single set of data (choose two options)
ii.   Non-parametric test for comparing 2 groups or 2 sets of data (choose two options)
iii. Non-parametric test to describe single set of data (choose two options)
iv.   Parametric test for comparing more than 2 groups (choose one option)
v.   Non-parametric test for comparing more than 2 groups (choose one option)

188-191 – *Cardiac effects of antidepressants*

Options

A.   TCAs
B.   Venlafaxine
C.   MAOIs
D.   SSRI
E.   Reboxetine
F.   Duloxetine
G.   Trazodone
H.   Mirtazapine

Lead in: Match the most appropriate set of cardiac effects profile from below with the most appropriate antidepressant drug from the above list.

Each option might be used once, more than once, or not at all.
i.   Increase in heart rate, prolongation of QTc interval and blocks cardiac Na/K channels (choose one option)
ii.   Significant increase in heart rate, can cause rhythm

abnormalities, atrial and ventricular ectopic beats, especially in elderly (choose <u>one</u> option)

iii. Slight increase in heart rate, no effect on QTc, caution in patients with recent MI and hypertension (choose <u>one</u> option)

iv. Minimal change in heart rate or blood pressure, no effect on QTc (choose <u>one</u> option)

192-196 – Antipsychotic drugs classification

Options

    A. Haloperidol
    B. Clozapine
    C. Risperidone
    D. Amisulpride
    E. Trifluperazine
    F. Flupenthixol
    G. Quetiapine
    H. Sulpride

Lead in: Choose the appropriate antipsychotic drugs from the above list for each of the following groups.

Each option might be used once, more than once, or not at all.

    i.   Thioxanthines (choose <u>one</u> option)
    ii. Dibenzothiazepine (choose <u>one</u> option)
    iii. Substituted benzamides (choose <u>two</u> options)
    iv. Bytyrophenones (choose <u>one</u> option)

197-200 – Neurotransmitters and psychiatric disorders

Options

    A. Histamine
    B. 5-hydroxytryptamine (5-HT)
    C. Dopamine (DA)
    D. Acetylcholine (ACh)
    E. Noradrenaline (NA)
    F. Gamma-aminobutyric acid (GABA)

G. Adrenaline
H. None of the above

Lead in: For each of the following psychiatric disorders, choose the most appropriate neurotransmitters from the above options. **Each option might be used once, more than once, or not at all.**

  i.   Obsessive Compulsive Disorder (OCD) (choose <u>one</u> option)
  ii. Parkinson's disease (choose <u>one</u> option)
  iii. Huntington's disease (choose <u>one</u> option)
  iv. Alzheimer's disease (choose <u>one</u> option)

Chapter 15b - mock answers

1. E

2. C

3. B

4. D

5. E

6. C – Cost utility analysis is preferred when there are multiple objectives of a program; for example, when quality of life and quantity of life are both important outcomes.

7. D

8. D

9. A

10. C

11. D – Interviewer bias is a type of observation bias.

12. C – Neyman bias is a type of sampling bias. Obsequiousness bias is a subtype of recall bias.

13. D – Randomisation is the only reliable way of avoiding selection bias.

14. C – Per-protocol analysis is an approach in which data from only those patients who complied with the trial protocol are included in the analysis. It can, however, introduce bias.

15. B

16. B

17. B

18. E

19. A

20. D

21. A
Wood, L S, *et al.*: *Biol Psychiatry* 15, 61 (10): 1195-1199. May 2007.

22. B

23. D

24. B

25. C
G D Schellenberg, *et al.*: *Molecular Psychiatry* 11: 1049-1060. 2006.

26. B
Gasperoni, T L, *et al.*: Genetic linkage and association between chromosome 1q and working memory function in schizophrenia. *Am J Med Genet* 116 (1 suppl): 8-16. 2003.

27. C

28. B

B   D

30. B
John Potokar, Michael Thase: *Advances in the Management and Treatment of Depression.* 2005.

31. A

32. B
Gray, *et al.*: 1997.

33. B

34. B

35. D
Wood, L S, *et al.*: *Biol Psychiatry* 15, 61 (10): 1195-1199. May 2007.

36. B

37. E

38. C
   Molecular Psychiatry 10: 563-571. 2005.

39. A
   Semple, D, *et al*.: *Oxford Handbook of Psychiatry*. 2005.

40. C

41. B – The septum is located in the middle anteroventral cerebrum and is composed of medium-size neurons grouped into medial, lateral and posterior groups. The septal nuclei have efferent connections with stria medullaris thalami and hypothalamus. Their afferent connections are from the olfactory tract, amygdala, cingulate gyrus and brainstem. The septum also has a reciprocal connection with hippocampus and habenula.
   The septal nuclei play an important role in reward and reinforcement.

42. E - Raphe nuclei, nucleus coeruleus, tuberomammillary nucleus and midbrain cholinergic nuclei maintain arousal, whereas lateral hypothalamus promotes arousal. The flip-flop influence of hypothalamus on the brainstem mechanisms regulates sleep-wake cycle and REM-NREM cycle within sleep. Ventrolateral preoptic nucleus promotes sleep.

   Gilmartin & Thomas: Mechanisms of arousal from sleep and their consequences. *Curr Opin Pulm Med* 10 (6): 468-474. 2004.

43. D – Dreams can occur in both rapid eye movement (REM) and non-rapid eye movement (NREM) sleep. They are, however, more frequent and easy to recall in REM sleep. Factors such as salience and level of arousal also have a role to play in dream recall. There is higher brain activity in the limbic system than the frontal cortex during dreams and the contents are more emotional than real life.
   Lucid dreaming is the conscious perception of one's state while dreaming. In this state a person usually has control over characters and the environment of the dream as well as his own actions within the dream.

Watanabe, T: Lucid Dreaming: Its Experimental Proof and Psychological Conditions. *J Int Soc Life Inf Sci* 21 (1). 2003.

44. **A** – There are 5 stages of a sleep cycle. Stages 1-4 are NREM sleep, whereas stage 5 is REM sleep. EEG shows theta rhythm in stages 1-4; however, in addition, spindles and K complexes are present in stage 2, and delta rhythm in stages 3 and 4. Beta rhythm is seen in stage 5. It takes about one hour to descend through stages 1-4, which is followed by several minutes of REM sleep. There are several such cycles per average sleep period. Muscle tone is moderately low in stages 1-4, whereas it is very low in REM sleep, which is referred to as REM atonia. This prevents dreams resulting in dangerous body movements.

Benbadis, S R: 'Introduction to EEG'. In: Lee-Chiong T, ed: *Sleep: A Comprehensive Handbook*, pp 989-1024. Hoboken, NJ: Wiley & Sons. 2006.

45. **E** – It can be very difficult at times to distinguish a seizure from a pseudoseizure. This is because often patients have both. Factors which are suggestive of seizure include relation to sleep deprivation, sudden onset and termination, injuries sustained during seizure, incontinence, impaired reflexes and increased prolactin levels at 15 minute post-seizure. Prolactin levels are only of value if you have a baseline available as in a psychiatric setting patients may have a raised prolactin secondary to antipsychotic medication use.

    Pseudoseizure usually occurs in the presence of an audience with a gradual onset and termination. It is generally triggered by interpersonal stress. Seizure is exacerbated by restraint and is characterised by bizarre purposeful movements, during which consciousness is preserved. However, most of them close their eyes during their 'seizure'. Patients with pseudoseizure tend to have positive findings on Minnesota Multiphasic Personality Inventory (MMPI), suggesting that they may have an 'epileptic personality'.

Dale J Shaw: Differential MMPI performance in pseudo-seizure epileptic and pseudo-neurologic groups. *J Clin Psych* 22 (3): 271-275. 2006.

46. **D** – Depression affects almost half of all people with Parkinson's disease. It isn't a dismayed reaction to Parkinson's disease. Rather, it's part of the illness and usually presents before onset of motor symptoms. The diagnosis is not easy because clinical symptoms of depression can overlap with or be mistaken for those of Parkinson's disease (such as the flat affect, inability to

work, fatigue, preoccupation with ill health, loss of desire, and reduction in libido). Moreover, depression in patients with Parkinson's disease is qualitatively different from primary major depression in that self-blame, guilt, delusions, a sense of failure, self-destructive thoughts, and suicide are less frequent. The severity of depression contributes to the cognitive disorders in Parkinson's disease; in patients with Parkinson's disease who do not have dementia, depression is associated with a significantly increased risk of developing dementia.

Allain, H, *et al.*: Depression in Parkinson's Disease. *BMJ* 320: 1287-1288. 2000.

47. **C** – Pick's disease is a type of frontotemporal dementia. It has several unique biochemical characteristics that allow for unique identification of Pick's disease as opposed to other pathological subtypes of frontotemporal dementia. The most striking of these is that this disease, which has tau protein tangles present in many affected neurons, contains only one or as many as two of the six different isoforms of the tau protein. Clinically it presents with early loss of social skills and executive functions with personality changes. Patients usually have naming deficits, echolalia, impaired auditory comprehension and poverty of speech, sometimes to the point of mutism. Memory and visuospatial skills are relatively spared. Some patients may have transient depression, one third has elation of mood and less than a third will have delusions.

Iskei & Arai: Progress in the classification of non-Alzheimer-type degenerative dementias. *Psychogeriatrics* 6 (1): 41-42. 2006.

48. **A** – Lewy body dementia is a neurodegenerative disorder resulting in slowly progressive and unrelenting dementia until death. Prevalence studies suggest that it is the second most common dementing illness in the elderly. The neuropathologic findings of Lewy body dementia show a wide anatomic range. Lewy bodies and Lewy-related pathology are found from the brainstem to the cortex and, in many cases, are associated with concurrent Alzheimer's disease pathology. A recent international consortium on Lewy body dementia has resulted in revised criteria for the clinical and pathological diagnosis of Lewy body dementia incorporating new information about the core clinical features and improved methods for their assessment. The presentation of Lewy body dementia is typically one of cortical and subcortical cognitive impairments, with worse visuospatial and executive dysfunction than Alzheimer's disease. There may

be relative sparing of memory, especially in the early stages. Core clinical features of Lewy body dementia include fluctuating attention, recurrent visual hallucinations, and Parkinsonism. Suggestive features include REM sleep behaviour disorder, severe neuroleptic sensitivity, and low dopamine transporter uptake in the basal ganglia on functional neuroimaging. Additional supportive features that commonly occur in Lewy body dementia, but with lower specificity, include repeated falls and syncope, transient, unexplained loss of consciousness, severe autonomic dysfunction, hallucinations in other modalities, systematised delusions, depression, relative preservation of medial temporal lobe structures on structural neuroimaging, reduced occipital activity on functional neuroimaging, prominent slow wave activity on electroencephalogram, and low uptake myocardial scintigraphy. Management of Lewy body dementia includes pharmacological and non-pharmacological interventions for its cognitive, neuropsychiatric, motor, and sleep disturbances.

Weisman & McKeith: Dementia with Lewy bodies. *Semin Neurol* 27 (1): 42-47. 2007.

49. **B** – Wilson's disease is an autosomal recessive disease. It is caused by a gene defect on chromosome 13 coding for protein used in copper metabolism. Copper accumulates to toxic levels in liver, cornea and basal ganglia, causing symptoms by age 20-30 years. Copper deposition causes a cavitary necrosis of the putamen and atrophy of the brainstem and dentate nucleus. Psychiatric symptoms correlate to neurological dysfunction rather than liver disease. Males and females are equally affected. Psychiatric symptoms include mild memory and executive disturbances. About one third develop depression but some may have mania or hypomania. Personality changes can present as impulsivity, irritability and lability. Motor symptoms usually present first and include tremor, rigidity, dystonia, poor co-ordination, abnormal gait and posture, dysarthria, dysphagia and hypophonia. The classic eye sign is Kayser-Fleischer rings, green copper deposits in the cornea. Wilson's disease should be suspected in young patients with movement disorder.

Constantine, G: 'Brain Tumours, Systemic Lupus Erythematosus, HIV/AIDS and Wilson's Disease'. In *Psychiatric Aspects of Neurologic Diseases: Practical Approaches to Patient Care*. Eds: Constantine, G, *et al*. Oxford University Press, US. 2007.

50. **B** – Fahr's disease or Familial idiopathic basal ganglia calcification

is a neurodegenerative disorder with characteristic calcium deposits in the basal ganglia and other brain areas visualised on neuroimaging. It is an autosomal dominant disease. Most affected individuals are in good health during childhood and young adulthood and typically present in the third to fifth decade, with gradually progressive neuropsychiatric and movement disorders. The first manifestations often include clumsiness, fatigability, unsteady gait, slow or slurred speech, dysphagia, involuntary movements, or muscle cramping. Seizures of various types occur frequently. Neuropsychiatric symptoms, often the first or most prominent manifestations, range from mild difficulty with concentration and memory to changes in personality and/ or behaviour, to psychosis and dementia. There is no correlation between the age of onset and extent of calcification.

Manyam, B V: What is and what is not 'Fahr's disease'. *Parkinsonism Relat Disord* 11: 73-80. 2005.

51. **D** – Huntington's disease is an autosomal dominant disease with complete penetrance. Degeneration begins in the medial caudate nucleus, the degree of degeneration correlates with degree of cognitive dysfunction, and proceeds laterally to the putamen. Somatostatin levels are increased, whereas GABA and acetylcholine levels in the striatum are decreased. Initial motor symptoms include mild rigidity and tic-like jerks which deteriorate by emotional distress and sleep deprivation. They also develop writhing movements, grimacing, head-bobbing and dancing gait. The majority of patients develop psychiatric symptoms before the onset of cognitive or motor symptoms. One third will develop depression. Substance misuse is not common than in general population. The leading causes of death, which usually occurs approximately 14 years after diagnosis, are pneumonia, trauma and suicide.

Gillian Bates, Peter Harper, and Lesley Jones: *Huntington's Disease*. 3rd ed. Oxford: Oxford University Press. 2002.

52. **C** – High premorbid intelligence and preserved olfaction are good prognostic indicators for recovery from traumatic brain injury; whereas increased age, intoxication, chronic substance misuse, learning disability, past psychiatric history, pre-existing behaviour problems and long post-traumatic amnesia are poor prognostic indicators.

Zink, B J: Traumatic brain injury outcome: Concepts for emergency care. *Ann Emerg Med* 37 (3): 318-332. 2001.

53. **E** – HIV directly affects temporolimbic structures, the thalamus and basal ganglia. Neurons are not directly targeted; however, they get affected indirectly due to neurotoxicity caused by irreversible binding of gp120 protein in viral capsid to the calcium channels increasing intracellular calcium. The consequent extensive cerebral atrophy manifests as enlarged ventricles instead of widened sulci.

Catani, M, *et al.*: gp120 induces cell death in human neuroblastoma cells through the CXCR4 and CCR5 chemokine receptors. *J Neurochem* 74 (6): 2373-2379. 2000.

54. **A** – Delirium is common and difficult to treat. Incidence of depression is about one third, with history of depression being a risk factor. Suicidal ideation is present in about half of the cases. Mania and anxiety may occur as a side effect of zidovudine. Anxiety could also be triggered by knowledge of diagnosis and CNS infections.

Constantine, G: 'Brain Tumours, Systemic Lupus Erythematosus, HIV/AIDS and Wilson's Disease'. In *Psychiatric Aspects of Neurologic Diseases: Practical Approaches to Patient Care*. Eds: Constantine, G, *et al.* Oxford University Press, US. 2007.

55. **E** – Cognitive impairment is present in about a third of patients. It is of two types; firstly, recognition memory loss associated with present or past CNS involvement, and secondly, impaired short-term memory and concentration associated with systemic disease activity. Psychiatric symptoms include depression, anxiety, alcohol abuse and psychosis. Suicidality is increased during active disease and is associated with diffusely slow EEG waves. Both cognitive and psychiatric symptoms fluctuate with the activity of disease. However, irritability and apathy are independent of disability and chronic disease and represent unique disease manifestations.

Constantine, G: 'Brain Tumours, Systemic Lupus Erythematosus, HIV/AIDS and Wilson's Disease'. In *Psychiatric Aspects of Neurologic Diseases: Practical Approaches to Patient Care*. Eds: Constantine, G, *et al.* Oxford University Press, US. 2007.

56. **D** - The first symptom of CJD is rapidly progressive dementia, leading to memory loss, personality changes and hallucinations. This is accompanied by speech impairment, myoclonus, ataxia, rigid posture, and seizures. The duration of the disease varies greatly, but sporadic CJD can be fatal within months or even weeks.

CSF analysis reveals raised 14-3-3 protein. EEG shows characteristic triphasic spikes. On T2-weighted images MRI shows high signal intensity in the caudate nucleus and putamen bilaterally. Diffusion Weighted Imaging (DWI) images are the most sensitive. In about 24% of cases DWI shows only cortical hyperintensity; in 68%, cortical and subcortical abnormalities; and in 5%, only subcortical anomalies.

Young, G S, *et al*.: Diffusion-Weighted and Fluid-Attenuated Inversion Recovery Imaging in Creutzfeldt-Jakob Disease: High Sensitivity and Specificity for Diagnosis. *American Journal of Neuroradiology* 26: 1551-1562. 2005.

57. **A** - Friedreich ataxia, an autosomal recessive neurodegenerative disease, is the most common of the inherited ataxias. The discovery of the gene that is mutated in this condition, FRDA, has led to rapid advances in the understanding of the pathogenesis of Friedreich ataxia. About 98% of mutant alleles have an expansion of a GAA trinucleotide repeat in intron 1 of the gene. This leads to reduced levels of the protein, frataxin. There is mounting evidence to suggest that Friedreich ataxia is the result of accumulation of iron in mitochondria, leading to excess production of free radicals, which then results in cellular damage and death.

Delatycki, B, *et al*.: Friedreich ataxia: an overview. *J Med Genet* 37: 1-8. 2000.

58. **E** - Female gender is a risk factor.

59. **C**

60. **B** - Gelineau's syndrome is also known as Narcolepsy. Almost 100% of cases are linked with HLA-DR2 antigen.

61. **B**

62. **D**

63. **E**

64. **A**

65. **C**

66. **A**
67. **E**

68. C

69. B

70. A

71. D – Large family size is also associated with low intelligence and behavioural problems. Oldest child, however, has slight advantage in intellectual development. Having lesbian parents or extended family does not have any harmful effect on a child's development; however, having a single parent with little support may lead to emotional and behavioural problems.

72. B

73. C – In addition, low levels of authoritative parenting, high levels of family conflicts and stress, marital conflicts and harsh parenting from mothers to their ADHD sons is reported.

74. E

75. C

76. A – Retrograde amnesia is often temporally graded, meaning that remote memories are more easily accessible than events occurring just prior to the trauma; this is referred to as Ribot's Law.

77. E

78. A

79. D

80. C

81. C

82. E

83. E – Self-help manuals and psychoeduacation are useful as first step. IPT may be as effective as CBT in the long term, but takes longer to show response.

84. A

85. B

86. B – Visual hallucinations are the most frequent psychotic phenomena.

87. B – Flumazenil can be given only through intravenous route. It produces little pharmacological effect itself but blocks the actions of other benzodiazepines.

Gelder, M, Harrison, P & Cowen, P (eds): *Shorter Oxford Textbook of Psychiatry.* Oxford University Press, Oxford. 2006.

88. C – The half-life of Chlordiazepoxide is 5-30 hours but has an active benzodiazepine metabolite which has a half-life of 36-200 hours. The half-life of chlordiazepoxide increases significantly in the elderly, which may result in prolonged action as well as accumulation of the drug during repeated administration.

Ashton, H: *Benzodiazepine Abuse, Drugs and Dependence*, pp 197-212. Harwood Academic Publishers; Routledge, London & New York. 2002.

89. C – Venlafaxine is a serotonin-noradrenaline reuptake inhibitor (SNRI).

90. B – Amisulpride at higher doses is relatively selective for limbic rather than striatal areas, which translates clinically into low potential for EPSE.

Taylor, D, Paton, C, & Kerwin, R: *The Maudsley Prescribing Giudelines.* 9th ed. Informa Healthcare, London. 2007.

91. A – Paliperidone (9-OH risperidone) is the major active metabolite of risperidone.

Vermier, M, *et al.*: Absorption, metabolism and excreation of a single oral dose of 14C-paliperidone in healthy subjects. *Clin Pharmacol Ther* 79: 80. 2006.

92. D – Psychotropic drugs and their metabolites are excreted mainly through the kidney.

93. B – Weight gain with antipsychotic drugs is associated with an allele of the 5-HT2c receptor.

Gelder, M, Harrison, P, & Cowen, P (eds): *Shorter Oxford Textbook of Psychiatry.* Oxford University Press, Oxford. 2006.

94. **A** – The current evidence suggests that it may be effective in the treatment of mild depression only. It is not a licensed medicine in the UK, but is available as a herbal and complementary therapy.

Linde, K, *et al.*: St John's wort for depression: meta-analysis of randomised controlled trails. *Br J Psychiatry* 186: 99-107. 2005.

95. **D** – Leucopoenia can happen rarely. Other adverse effects are insomnia, agitation, tremor, mania, confusion, oedema, rashes, hepatocellular toxicity (rare) and autonomic side effects.

Gelder, M, Harrison, P & Cowen, P (eds): *Shorter Oxford Textbook of Psychiatry*. Oxford University Press, Oxford. 2006.

96. **D** – Mirtazapine, SSRIs (except citalopram), MAOIs, Reboxetine, valproate, benzodiazepines, lamotrigine, gabapentin and carbamezapine have no effects on QTc prolongation.

Stollberger, C, et al.: Antipsychotic drugs and QT prolongation. *Int Clin Psychopharmacol* 20: 243-251. 2005

97. **B** – Plasma level can be expected to fall by 0.2 mmol/l between 12 and 24 hours post-dose.

Perlis, R H, *et al.*: Effect of abrupt change from standard to low serum levels of lithium; a reanalysis of double blind lithium maintenance data. *AM J Psychiatry* 159: 1155-1159. 2002.

98. **C** – Bupropion does not cause sexual dysfunction. Its adverse effects profile is similar to SSRIs. Insomnia, tremor, agitation and nausea have been reported frequently.

Gelder, M, Harrison, P, & Cowen, P (eds): *Shorter Oxford Textbook of Psychiatry*. Oxford University Press, Oxford. 2006.

99. **E** – Mianserin is a quadricyclic compound. It is a weak inhibitor of noradrenaline reuptake and antagonises different 5HT receptors, particularly 5 HT-2. It is also competitive antagonist at H-1, á1 and á2-adrenoceptors.

100. **C**

101. **A** – Haloperidol is associated with impotence and painful ejaculation.

Mulcahy, J J (ed): *Male Sexual Function A Guide to Clinical Management*. Humana Press. 2001.

102. D - Fluoxetine has a slower onset of antidepressants effect than other SSRIs. Escitalopram may be superior in efficacy compared with other SSRIs in the treatment of major depressive disorder. Also, escitalopram has better efficacy in the treatment of severe depression than citalopram.

Kennedy, S H, Andersen, H F, Lam, R W: Efficacy of escitalopram in the treatment of major depressive disorder compared with conventional selective serotonin reuptake inhibitors and venlafaxine XR: a meta-analysis. *J Psychiatry Neurosci* 31 (2): 122-131. 2006.

103. E - Trazadone's approved indication is major depressive disorder. Other 'off-label' uses include: insomnia, OCD, panic disorder, GAD and migraine.

Borras, L, de Timary, P, Constant, E L, Huguelet, P, Eytan, A: Successful treatment of alcohol withdrawal with trazodone. *Pharmacopsychiatry* 39 (6): 232. 2006.

Fink, H A, MacDonald, R, Rutks, I R, Wilt, T J: Trazodone for erectile dysfunction: a systematic review and meta-analysis. *BJU Int* 92 (4): 441-446. 2003.

104. C - Pipothiazine palmitate requires 8-12 weeks to reach steady state, 9-10 days to peak plasma level and needs to be administered every 4 weeks.

Gelder, M, Harrison, P, & Cowen, P (eds): *Shorter Oxford Textbook of Psychiatry.* Oxford University Press, Oxford. 2006.

105. B - Mirtazapine has only minor inhibitory effects on cytochrome P450 isoenzymes.

106. C - D2 receptor occupancy is 65% for clozapine, 75% for olanzapine and 80% for both chlorpromazine and aripiprazole.

107. D - Children of lone parents were about twice more likely to have a mental health problem than those living with married or cohabiting couples. Among all the sampled children, those in two-child households had the lowest rate of mental disorder (8%) compared with those who were part of four- and five-children households,13% and 18% respectively.
Meltzer, H, Gatward, R, Goodman, R, and Ford, T: *Mental Health of Children and Adolescents in Great Britain.* London: The Stationery Office. 2000.

108. D - For each type of disorder the rates for looked-after children compared with private household children were: emotional disorders 11% compared with 3%; conduct disorders 36% compared with 5%; and hyperkinetic disorders 11% compared with 2%.

Meltzer, H, et al: *The mental health of young people looked after by local authorities in England.* The Office for National Statistics (ONS). 2003.

109. D – 12.3% of the sample had borderline intelligence, according to DSM-IV criteria.

Hassiotis, A, Strydom, A, Hall, I: Psychiatric morbidity and social functioning among adults with borderline intelligence living in private households. *Journal of Intellectual Disability Research*, vol 52, no 2, pp 95-106 (12). February 2008.

110. B – It has a brief version (SPQ-B) with 22 items.

Axelrod, S R, Grilo, C M, Sanislow, C, & McGlashan, T H: Schizotypal Personality Questionnaire Brief: Factor structure and convergent validity in inpatient adolescents. *Journal of Personality Disorders* 15: 168-179. 2001.

111. D – PANSS has seven positive-symptom items, and seven negative-symptom items. The positive- and negative-symptom item groups are often reported separately, with a possible range of 7 to 49. A patient with schizophrenia entering a clinical trial typically scores 91.

Geddes, J, et al.: Atypical antipsychotics in the treatment of schizophrenia: systematic overview and meta-regression analysis. *BMJ* 321: 1371-1376. 2000.

112. C – The cross-sectional survey is an inefficient design for a rare disorder such as schizophrenia. Cross-sectional surveys can be used to measure the prevalence of a disorder within a population.

Prince, M: 'Epidemiology'. In Wright, P, Stern, J, & Phelen, M (eds): *Core Psychiatry*, 2nd ed. Elsevier Saunders. 2005.

113. C – 50% of the deaths are due to suicide in persons aged 20-35 years. Suicide is the second leading cause of death in this group.

114. C – It may account for 1-2% of psychiatric admissions.

Semple, D, et al. (eds): *Oxford Handbook of Psychiatry.* Oxford University Press. 2005.

115. A – 4% of psychiatric admissions are associated with it. One RCT support use of risperidone to treat it. The disorder tends to run a very stable course. It is classified along with cluster A/odd eccentric personality disorders in DSM-IV.

Koeningsberg, H W, *et al.*: Risperidone in the treatment of schizotypal disorder. *J Clin Psychiatry* 64: 628-634. 2003.

116. B – Parkinson's disease has typical onset in the 50s and peaks during the 70s.

117. B – There is 30 times increased risk of suicide in those infected with the virus.

118. B

119. A

120. E

121. D – There are several forms of psychotherapy, but mainly five principal kinds: Psychodynamic, Cognitive behavioural, Integrative, Systemic and Counselling.

122. D – Dream work is a process that converts latent dream into manifest dream. Examination of dreams is a technique used in dynamic psychotherapy where dreams are viewed as being formed as a mixture of daytime memories, nocturnal stimuli and unconscious desires. This admixture is called latent dream, which is converted to manifest dream by dream work. It's used to unravel unconscious desires.

123. B

Becker, D F, *et al.*: Diagnostic Efficiency of Borderline Personality Disorder Criteria in Hospitalised Adolescents: Comparison with Hospitalised Adults. *Am J Psychiatry*. 2002.

EMI – answers

124-130.
  i.   A, C
  ii.   A, G, I
  iii. B, G
131-134.
  i.   D
  ii.   E
  iii. A, B
135-138.
  i.   A, G
  ii.   K
  iii. J
139-141.
  i.   B
  ii.   I
  iii. C
142-144.
  i.   D
  ii.   A
  iii. F
145-149.
  i.   B, D
  ii.   A, F
  iii. H
150-162.
  i.   A, B, E, L
  ii.   C, G, H, K
  iii. C, D, F, I, J
163-168.
  i.   D, G – Angelman syndrome
  ii.   C, H – Williams syndrome
  iii. A, F – Huntington's disease
169-173.
  i.   A, D, F
  ii.   C
  iii. E
174-176.
  i.   G
  ii.   B
  iii. H

177-179.

- i.   G
- ii. C
- iii. A

180-187.

- i.   A, C
- ii. F, H
- iii. B, G
- iv. E
- v.   I

188-191.

- i.   A
- ii. E
- iii. F
- iv. H

192-196.

- i.   F
- ii. G
- iii. D, H
- iv. A

197-200.

- i.   B
- ii. C
- iii. F
- iv. D

Chapter 16 – References and further reading

1. Marangell, L B, et al.: A 1-Year Pilot Study of Vagus Nerve Stimulation in Treatment-Resistant Rapid-Cycling Bipolar Disorder. *J Clin Psychiatry* 69: 183-189. 2008.
2. Anderson, I M & Reid, I C: *Fundamentals of Clinical Psychopharmacology*, 2nd ed. Taylor & Francis, Abingdon, Oxon. 2004.
3. Gelder, M, Harrison, P & Cowen, P (eds): *Shorter Oxford Textbook of Psychiatry*. Oxford University Press, Oxford. 2006.
4. Gardner, D M, et al.: Modern antipsychotic drugs: a critical review. *CMAJ* 172: 1703-1711. 2005.
5. Tranulis, C, et al.: Somatic augmentation strategies in clozapine resistance – what facts? *Clin Neuropharmacol* 29: 34-44. 2006.
6. McGrath, P J, et al.: Tranylcypromine versus venlafaxine plus mirtazapine treatments for depression: a STAR* D report. *Am J Psychiatry* 163: 1519-1530. 2006.
7. Marder, S R, et al.: Aripiprazole in the treatment of schizophrenia: safety and tolerability in short-term, placebo-controlled trials. *Schizopher Res* 61: 123-136. 2003.
8. Kohen, D: Psychotropic medication and breast-feeding. *Advances in Psychiatric Treatment* 11: 371-379. 2005.
9. Taylor, D, Paton, C & Kerwin, R: *The Maudsley Prescribing Giudelines*, 9th ed. Informa Healthcare, London. 2007.
10. Lattanzi, L, et al.: Subcutaneous apomorphine for neuroleptic malignant syndrome. *Am J Psychiatry* 163: 1450-1451. 2006.
11. Von Moltke, L L, et al. : *Psychotropic Drug Metabolism in Old Age: Principles and Problems of Assessment*. 2000.
12. Gillman, P: Comment on: Serotonin syndrome due to co-administration of linezolid and venlafaxine. *J Antimicrob Chemother* 54 (4): 844–845. 2004.
13. Boyer, E W, Shannon, M: The serotonin syndrome. *N Engl J Med* 352 (11): 1112–1120. 2005.
14. Iqbal, M M et al.: Clozapine: a clinical review of adverse effects and management. *Ann Clin Psychiatry* 15: 33–48. 2003.
15. Spina, E, et al.: Clinical significance of pharmacokinetic interactions between anti-epileptic and psychotropic drugs. *Epelepsia* 42 (Suppl 2): 37-44. 2002.
16. Bazire, S: *Psychtropic Drug Directory: The Professionals' Pocket Handbook and Aide Memoire*. Salisbury: Fivepen. 2005.
17. Anderson, I M & Reid, I C: *Fundamentals of Clinical Psychopharmacology*, 2nd ed. Taylor & Francis, Abingdon, Oxon. 2004.
18. Taylor, M J, Freemantle, N, Geddes, J R, et al.: Early onset of selective serotonin reuptake inhibitor antidepressant action: systematic review and meta-analysis. *Arch Gen Psychiatry* 63: 1217–1223. 2006.
19. Appolinario, J C, et al.: Psychotropic drugs in the treatment of obesity. What promise? *CNS Drugs* 18: 629-651. 2004.
20. *Pharmacotherapy* 23(6): 811-815. Pharmacotherapy Publications. 2003.
21. Køenová, M & Pelclová, D: A 4-year study of lithium intoxication reported to the Czech Toxicological Information Centre. *Pharmacy World and Science* 28: 5, pp 274-277 (4). 2006.
22. Katzenschlager, R, Sampaio, C, Costa, J, et al.: Anticholinergics for symptomatic management of Parkinson's disease. *The Cochrane Database of Systematic Reviews*, issue 3. 2002.
23. Arnold, L M, Lu, Y, Crofford, L J, et al. : A double-blind, multicenter trial comparing duloxetine with placebo in the treatment of fibromyalgia patients with or without

major depressive disorder. *Arthritis Rheum* 50: 2974-2984. 2004.

24. Millard, R J, Moore, K, Rencken, R, Yalcin, I, Bump, R C: Duloxetine UI Study Group. Duloxetine vs placebo in the treatment of stress urinary incontinence: a four-continent randomized clinical trial. *BJU Int* 93(3): 311-318. 2004.

25. Gulseren, L, *et al*.: Comparasion of flouxetine and paroxetine in type 2 diabetes mellitus patients. *Arch Med Res* 36: 159-65. 2005.

26. National Institute for Health and Clinical Excellence: Bipolar disorder. The management of bipolar disorder in adults, children and adolescents, in primary and secondary care. Clinical guidance 38. http://www.nice.org.uk. 2006.

27. Crossman & Neary: Introduction and overview. In *Neuroanatomy, an illustrated colour text*. 2nd ed. 2000.

28. Oktar, *et al*.: Blood flow volume quantification in internal carotid and vertebral arteries: comparison of 3 different ultrasound techniques with phase contrast MR imaging. *AJNR Am J Neuroradiol*. 2006.

29. McCaffrey, P: The Neuroscience on the Web Series: CMSD 620 Neuroanatomy of Speech, Swallowing and Language. 2008.

30. McCaffrey, P: The Neuroscience on the Web Series: CMSD 620 Neuroanatomy of Speech, Swallowing and Language. 2008.

31. Quentin, S: Transport of Glutamate and Other Amino Acids at the Blood Brain Barrier. *Journal of Nutrition* 130: 1016S-1022S. 2000.

32. Nolte, J: *The Human Brain: An introduction to its Functional Anatomy*. 5th ed. 2002.

33. Crossman & Neary: Introduction and overview. In *Neuroanatomy, an illustrated colour text*. 2nd ed. 2000.

34. Manto & Pandolfo: *The Cerebellum and Its Disorders*. New York: Cambridge University Press. 2001.

35. Schmahmann, J: Neuropsychiatric Practice and Opinion: Disorders of the Cerebellum: Ataxia, Dysmetria of Thought, and the Cerebellar Cognitive Affective Syndrome. *J Neuropsychiatry Clin Neurosci* 16: 367-378. August 2004.

36. Ligon, K, *et al*.: The oligodendroglial lineage marker OLIG2 is universally expressed in diffuse gliomas. *Journal of neuropathology and experimental neurology*. vol. 63, no 5, pp 499-509 [11 page(s) (article)] (48 ref). 2004.

37. Purves, D, *et al*.: 'The Organization of the Nervous System'. In *Neuroscience*. 2nd ed. 2001.

38. Percheron, G: 'Thalamus'. In Paxinos, G and May, J (eds). *The Human Nervous System*. 2nd ed, pp 592-675. 2003.

39. Roselli, C, *et al*.: Volume of a Sexually Dimorphic Nucleus in the Ovine Medial Preoptic Area/Anterior Hypothalamus Varies with Sexual Partner Preference. *Endocrinology* 145 (2): 478–483. 2004.

40. Greenstein, B: Introduction. In *Concise Clinical Pharmacology. Idiopathic Parkinson's disease I*. Published by Pharmaceutical Press. 2007.

41. Bonnet & Houeto: Pathophysiology of Parkinson's Disease. *Biomedicine & Pharmacotherapy* 53 (3):117-121. 1999.

42. Berardelli, A, *et al*.: Pathophysiology of chorea and bradykinesia in Huntington's disease. *Movement Disorders* 14 (3): 398-403. .2001.

43. Hoyer, D, *et al*.: International Union of Pharmacology classification of receptors for 5-hydroxytryptamine (Serotonin). *Pharmacol Rev* 46 (2): 157–203. .1994.

44. Van Diepen & Eickholt: Function of PTEN during the Formation and Maintenance of Neuronal Circuits in the Brain. *Dev Neurosci* 30: 59-64. 2008.

45. Pilarski & Eng: Will the real Cowden syndrome please stand up (again)? Expanding mutational and clinical spectra of the PTEN hamartoma tumour syndrome. *J Med Genet* 41 (5): 323–326. 2004.

46. Stern, J M, Engel, J: *An Atlas of EEG Patterns*. Philadelphia: Lippincott Williams & Wilkins. 2004.

47. Kandel, E, *et al*.: *Principles of Neural Science*. Mcgraw-Hill Professional. 2000.

48. LeDoux, J: Emotion Circuits in the Brain. *Annual Review of Neuroscience* 23: 155-184.

2000.

49. Bear, M, et al.: Neuroscience: Exploring the Brain. 3rd ed, pp 568-569. Philadelphia, PA: Lippincott Williams & Wilkins. 2007.

50. Rosaleen A McCarthy: Semantic Knowledge and Semantic Representations. Psychology Press. 1995.

51. Mesulam, M M: 'The Human Frontal Lobes: Transcending the Default Mode through Continent Encoding'. In D T Stuss and R T Knight: Principles of Frontal Lobe Function, pp 8-30. Oxford. 2002.

52. Avillac, M, Deneve, S, Olivier, E, Pouget, A, Duhamel, J R: Reference frames for representing visual and tactile locations in parietal cortex. Nat Neurosci 8 (7): 941-949. 2005.

53. Roux, F, et al.: Writing, calculating, and finger recognition of the angular gyrus: a cortical stimulation study of Gerstmann syndrome. J Neurosurgery 99: 716–727. 2003.

54. Bofarton, J, et al.: The field defects of anterior temporal lobectomy: a quantitative reassessment of Meyer's Loop. Brain 128 (9): 2123 – 2133. September 2005.

55. Galetovic, D, et al.: Bilateral cortical blindness – Anton Syndrome: case report. Collegium Antropologicom 29(1). 2005.

56. Scepkowski & Cronin-Golomb: The Alien Hand: Cases, Categorizations, and Anatomical Correlates. Behavioural and Cognitive Neuroscience Reviews 2 (4): 261-277. 2003.

57. Pearce, J: The Locked-in syndrome. Br Med J (Clin Res Ed) 294 (6566): 198-199. 1987.

58. MacIver, M B: 'The Hippocampus'. In Neural Mechanisms of Anaesthesia. Eds Antognini, et al. Humana Press. 2002.

59. Wenk, G L: Neuropathologic changes in Alzheimer's disease. J Clin Psychiatry 64 Suppl 9: 7–10. 2003.

60. Steriade & Pare: 'The amygdala'. In Gating in Cerebral Networks. Cambridge University Press. 2007.

61. Hayman, LA, et al.: Klüver-Bucy syndrome after selective damage of the amygdala and its cortical connections. J Neuropsychiatry Clin Neurosci 10: 354-358. 1998.

62. McElliskem, J: Affective and Predatory Violence: a Bimodal Classification System of Human Aggression and Violence. Aggression & Violent Behavior (10): 1-30. 2004.

63. Christine Brown and Keith Lloyd: APT 7: 350-356. 2001.

64. Hugh McPherson: Pragmatic clinical trials. Complementary Therapies in Medicine 12, 136-140. 2004.

65. Grimes, A D: Bias and causal associations in observational research. Lancet vol 359, 248-252. Jan 2002.

66. Hugh McPherson: Pragmatic clinical trials. Complementary Therapies in Medicine 12, 136-140. 2004.

67. Nikulin, M S and Greenwood, P E: A Guide to Chi Squared Testing. New York: Wiley – Inter science. 1996.

68. Richard A Berk: Regression Analysis: A Constructive Critique. Sage Publications. 2004.

69. Semple, D, et al.: Oxford Handbook of Psychiatry. 2005.

70. Bewick, V, et al.: Statistics review 13: Receiver operating characteristic curves. Crit Care, doi: 10.1186/cc3000. 2004.

71. Jerald F Lawless: Statistical Models and Methods for Lifetime Data. 2nd ed. John Wiley and Sons, Hoboken. 2003.

72. Smith, et al.: 'Psychological Development'. In Atkinson & Hilgard's Introduction to Psychology. 14th ed. Graphic World Publishing Services, Thomson Wadsworth. 2003.

73. Shiner, R L: A developmental perspective on personality disorders: lessons from research on normal personality development in childhood and adolescence. J

Personal Disord 19 (2): 202-210. 2005.

74. Skodol, A E: Longitudinal course and outcome of personality disorders. *Psychiatr Clin North Am* 31 (3): 495-503,viii. 2008.

75. Mcleod, *et al*.: Examining the association between parenting and childhood anxiety: A meta-analysis. *Clinical Psychology Review* 27 (2), 155-172. 2007.

76. Belsky, J, et al.: Are There Long-Term Effects of Early Child Care? *Child Development* 78 (2), 681-701. 2007.

77. Rutter, M, *et al*.: *Research and Innovation on the Road to Modern Child Psychiatry.* RCPsych Publications. 2001.

78. Strohschein, L: Parental Divorce and Child Mental Health Trajectories. *Journal of Marriage and Family* 67 (5), 1286-1300. 2005.

79. Kovas, Y, *et al*.: Genetic Influences in Different Aspects of Language Development: The Etiology of Language Skills in 4.5-Year-Old Twins. *Child Development* 76 (3), 632-651. 2005.

80. Baumrind, D: Parental disciplinary patterns and social competence in children. *Youth and Society*, 9, 238-276. 1978.

81. Wicks, *et al*.: Social Adversity in Childhood and the Risk of Developing Psychosis: A National Cohort Study. *Am J Psychiatry* 162: 1652-1657. 2005.

82. Smith, *et al*.: 'Psychological Development'. In Atkinson & Hilgard's *Introduction to Psychology*. 14th ed. Graphic World Publishing Services, Thomson Wadsworth. 2003.

83. Schott, J M, *et al*.: Ischemic Bilateral Hippocampal Dysfunction During Transient Global Amnesia. *Neurology*,70 (20), 1940-1941. 2008.

84. Kopelman, M D: Disorders of memory. *Brain* 125: 2152-2190. 2002.

85. Isaac, C L, *et al*.: Is posttraumatic stress disorder associated with specific deficits in episodic memory? *Clin Psychol Rev* 26: 939-955. 2006.

86. Frodl, T S, *et al*.: Depression-Related Variation in Brain Morphology Over 3 Years, Effects of Stress? *Arch Gen Psychiatry* 65 (10): 1156-1165. 2008.

87. Huppert, F A, *et al*.: CAMCOG—a concise neuropsychological test to assist dementia diagnosis: socio-demographic determinants in an elderly population sample. *Br J Clin Psychol* 34 (Pt 4): 529 -541. 1995.

88. Schramm, U, *et al*.: Psychometric properties of Clock Drawing Test and MMSE or Short Performance Test in dementia screening in a memory clinic population. *Int J Geriatr Psychiatry* 17 (3): 254-260. 2002.

89. Kaplan & Saccuzzo: *Psychological Testing: Principles, applications and issues*. Thomson Wadsworth. 2005.

90. Loranger, A W: *International Personality Disorder Examination – IPDE Manual.* American Psychiatric Press. 1995.

91. Saulsman & Page: The five factor model and personality disorder empirical literature: A meta analytic review. *Clinical Psychology Review* 23, 1055-1085. 2004.

92. Sarkar & Adshead: Personality disorders as disorganisation of attachment and affect regulation. *Advances in Psychiatric Treatment* 12: 297-305. 2006.

93. Goldapple, K, *et al*.: Modulation of cortical-limbic pathways in major depression: treatment-specific effects of cognitive behavior therapy. *Arch Gen Psychiatry* 61: 34–41. 2004.

94. Davison & Tyrer: 'Psychosocial treatment in personality disorder'. In *Personality Disorders: diagnosis, management and cause.* Ed. Tyrer, P. Oxford: Butterworth Heinemann. 2000.

95. Ryle, A & Kerr, I B: *Introducing Cognitive Analytic Therapy: Principles and Practice.* Chichester: John Wiley & Sons. 2002.

96. Dimeff & Linehan: Dialectical behavior therapy in a nutshell. *The California Psychologist* 34: 10-13. 2001.

97. Markowitz, J: Evidence-Based Psychotherapies for Depression. *Journal of Occupational & Environmental Med* 50 (4): 437-440. 2008.

98. Young, J E, *et al*.: *Schema Therapy: A Practitioner's Guide.* Guildford Press. 2003.

99. Tyrer & Seivewright: 'Outcome of personality disorder'. In *Personality Disorders: diagnosis, management and cause*. Ed. Tyrer, P. Oxford: Butterworth Heinemann. 2000.

100. Anderson, I M & Reid, I C: *Fundamentals of Clinical Psychopharmacology*. 2nd ed. Taylor & Francis, Abingdon, Oxon. 2004.

101. Bymaster, F P, *et al.*: Fluoxetine, but not other selective serotonin uptake inhibitors, increases norepinephrine and dopamine extracellular levels in prefrontal cortex. *Psychopharmacology (Berl)* 160 (4): 353-361. 2002.

102. Owens, J M, Knight, D L, Nemeroff, C B: Second generation SSRIS: human monoamine transporter binding profile of escitalopram and R-fluoxetine. *Encephale* 28 (4): 350-355. 2002.

103. Taylor, D, Paton, C & Kerwin, R: *The Maudsley Prescribing Guidelines*. 9th ed. Informa Healthcare, London. 2007.

104. Hyland, K: Neurochemistry and defects of biogenic amine neurotransmitter metabolism. *J Inherit Metab Dis* 22, 353-363. 1999.

105. Girault & Greengard: The neurobiology of dopamine signaling. *Arch Neurol* 61 (5): 641-644. 2004.

106. Labuguen, R: Initial Evaluation of Vertigo. *Am Fam Physician* 73: 244-51, 254. 2006.

107. Luck, S. *An Introduction to the Event-related Potential Technique*. MIT Press. 2005.

108. Krakow, K, *et al.*: EEG recording during fMRI experiments: image quality. *Hum Brain Mapp* 10, 10± 15. 2000.

109. Wood, L S, et al.: *Biol Psychiatry* 15, 61 (10): 1195–1199. May 2007.

110. G D Schellenberg, *et al.*: *Molecular Psychiatry* 11, 1049–1060. 2006.

111. Gasperoni, T L, *et al.*: Genetic linkage and association between chromosome 1q and working memory function in schizophrenia. *Am J Med Genet* 116 (1 suppl): 8-16. 2003.

112. John Potokar, Michael Thase: *Advances in the management and Treatment of Depression*. 2005.

113. Wood, L S, *et al.*: *Biol Psychiatry*, 15; 61 (10): 1195-1199. May 2007.

114. Molecular Psychiatry 10, 563-571. 2005.

115. Gilmartin & Thomas: Mechanisms of arousal from sleep and their consequences. *Curr Opin Pulm Med* 10 (6): 468–474. 2004.

116. Watanabe, T: Lucid Dreaming: Its Experimental Proof and Psychological Conditions. *J Int Soc Life Inf Sci* 21 (1). 2003.

117. Benbadis, S R: 'Introduction to EEG'. In: Lee-Chiong, T, ed. *Sleep: A Comprehensive Handbook*, 989-1024. Hoboken, NJ: Wiley & Sons. 2006.

118. Dale J Shaw: Differential MMPI performance in pseudo-seizure epileptic and pseudo-neurologic groups. *J Clin Psych* 22 (3): 271-275. 2006.

119. Allain, H, *et al.*: Depression in Parkinson's Disease. *BMJ* 320: 1287-1288. 2000.

120. Iskei & Arai: Progress in the classification of non-Alzheimer-type degenerative dementias. *Psychogeriatrics* 6 (1): 41-42. 2006.

121. Weisman & McKeith: Dementia with Lewy bodies. *Semin Neurol* 27 (1): 42-47. 2007.

122. Constantine, G: 'Brain Tumours, Systemic Lupus Erythematosus, HIV/AIDS and Wilson's Disease'. In *Psychiatric Aspects of Neurologic Diseases: Practical Approaches to Patient Care*. Eds Constantine, G, *et al.* Oxford University Press, US. 2007.

123. Manyam, B V: What is and what is not 'Fahr's disease'. *Parkinsonism Relat Disord* 11: 73–80. 2005.

124. Gillian Bates, Peter Harper, and Lesley Jones: *Huntington's Disease*. 3rd ed. Oxford: Oxford University Press. 2002.

125. Zink, B J: Traumatic brain injury outcome: Concepts for emergency care. *Ann Emerg Med* 37 (3): 318–332. 2001.

126. Catani, M, *et al.*: gp120 induces cell death in human neuroblastoma cells through the CXCR4 and CCR5 chemokine receptors. *J Neurochem* 74 (6): 2373-2379. 2000.

127. Constantine, G: 'Brain Tumours, Systemic Lupus Erythematosus, HIV/AIDS and Wilson's Disease'. In *Psychiatric Aspects of Neurologic Diseases: Practical Approaches to Patient Care*. Eds Constantine, G, *et al*. Oxford University Press, US. 2007.

128. Young, G S, *et al*.: Diffusion-Weighted and Fluid-Attenuated Inversion Recovery Imaging in Creutzfeldt-Jakob Disease: High Sensitivity and Specificity for Diagnosis. *American Journal of Neuroradiology* 26: 1551-1562. 2005.

129. Delatycki, B, *et al*.: Friedreich ataxia: an overview. *J Med Genet* 37: 1-8. 2000.

130. Gelder, M, Harrison, P & Cowen, P (eds): *Shorter Oxford Textbook of Psychiatry*. Oxford University Press, Oxford. 2006.

131. Ashton, H: *Benzodiazepine Abuse, Drugs and Dependence*, pp 197-212. Harwood Academic Publishers; Routledge, London & New York. 2002.

132. Vermier, M, et al.: Absorption, metabolism and excreation of a single oral dose of 14C-paliperidone in healthy subjects. *Clin Pharmacol Ther* 79: 80. 2006.

133. Linde, K, *et al*.: St John's wort for depression: meta-analysis of randomised controlled trails. *Br J Psychiatry* 186: 99-107. 2005.

134. Stollberger, C, *et al*.: Antipsychotic drugs and QT prolongation. *Int Clin Psychopharmacol* 20: 243-251. 2005.

135. Perlis, R H, *et al*.: Effect of abrupt change from standard to low serum levels of lithium; a reanalysis of double blind lithium maintenance data. *AM J Psychiatry* 159: 1155-1159. 2002.

136. Mulcahy, J J (ed): *Male Sexual Function – A Guide to Clinical Management*. Humana Press. 2001.

137. Kennedy, S H, Andersen, H F, Lam, R W: Efficacy of escitalopram in the treatment of major depressive disorder compared with conventional selective serotonin reuptake inhibitors and venlafaxine XR: a meta-analysis. *J Psychiatry Neurosci* 31 (2): 122-131. 2006.

138. Borras, L, de Timary, P, Constant, E L, Huguelet, P, Eytan, A: Successful treatment of alcohol withdrawal with trazodone. *Pharmacopsychiatry* 39 (6): 232. 2006.

139. Fink, H A, MacDonald, R, Rutks, I R, Wilt, T J. Trazodone for erectile dysfunction: a systematic review and meta-analysis. *BJU Int* 92 (4): 441-446. 2003.

140. Meltzer, H, Gatward, R, Goodman, R and Ford, T: *Mental Health of Children and Adolescents in Great Britain*. London: The Stationery Office. 2000.

141. Meltzer, H, *et al*.: *The mental health of young people looked after by local authorities in England*. The Office for National Statistics (ONS). 2003.

142. Hassiotis, A, Strydom, A, Hall, I: Psychiatric morbidity and social functioning among adults with borderline intelligence living in private households. *Journal of Intellectual Disability Research*, vol 52, No 2, pp 95-106 (12). February 2008.

143. Axelrod, S R, Grilo, C M, Sanislow, C, & McGlashan, T H: Schizotypal Personality Questionnaire – Brief: Factor structure and convergent validity in inpatient adolescents. *Journal of Personality Disorders* 15, 168-179. 2001.

144. Geddes, J, *et al*.: Atypical antipsychotics in the treatment of schizophrenia: systematic overview and meta-regression analysis. *BMJ* 321: 1371-1376. 2000.

145. Prince, M: 'Epidemiology'. In Wright, P, Stern, J & Phelen, M (eds): *Core Psychiatry*, 2nd ed. Elsevier Saunders. 2005.

146. Semple, D, *et al*. (eds): *Oxford Handbook of Psychiatry*. Oxford University Press. 2005.

147. Koeningsberg, H W, *et al*.: Risperidone in the treatment of schizotypal disorder. *J Clin Psychiatry* 64: 628-634. 2003.

148. Becker, D F, *et al*.: Diagnostic Efficiency of Borderline Personality Disorder Criteria in Hospitalised Adolescents: Comparison with Hospitalised Adults. *Am J Psychiatry*. 2002.

149. NINDS fact sheet.

150. Spillantini, M G: The alpha-synucleinopathies: Parkinson's disease, dementia with Lewy bodies, and multiple system atrophy. *Ann N Y Acad Sci* 920: 16-27. 2000.

151. Duan, *et al*.: *Cell* 130: 1- 13. September 21, 2007.

152. Zeshan, Ahmed, *et al.*: Progranulin in frontotemporal lobar degeneration and neuroinflammation. *Journal of Neuroinflammation* 4: 7. 2007.
153. Harrison, P J, *et al.*: Schizophrenia genes, gene expression, and neuropathology. *Mol Psychiatry* 10 (1): 40-68. Jan 2005.
154. Irving I Gottesman, *et al.*: The Endophenotype Concept in Psychiatry. *Am J Psychiatry* 160: 636-645. April 2003.
155. Irving I Gottesman *et al.*: The Endophenotype Concept in Psychiatry. *Am J Psychiatry* 160: 636-645, April 2003.
156. National Organisation for Rare Disorders. 2005.
157. Tyrone D Cannon, Matthew C Keller: Endophenotypes in the Genetic Analyses of Mental Disorders, *Annual Review of Clinical Psychology*, vol 2, pp 267-290. April 2006.
158. Irving I Gottesman, *et al.*: The Endophentype Concept in Psychiatry. *Am J Psychiatry* 160: 636-645. April 2003.
159. Lara Menies, *et al.*: Neurocognitive endophenotypes of obsessive-compulsive disorder. *Brain*, doi: 10.1093/brain/awm205. Sept 2007.
160. David H Skuse: *The British Journal of Psychiatry* 178: 395-396. 2001.
161. Gasperoni, T L, *et al.*: Genetic linkage and association between chromosome 1q and working memory function in schizophrenia. *Am J Med Genet* 116 (1 suppl): 8-16. 2003.
162. Thapar, A, *et al.*: Gene–environment interplay in attention-deficit hyperactivity disorder and the importance of a developmental perspective. *BJP* 190: 1-3. 2007.
163. T Venkon, *et al.*: *Molecular Psychiatry* 13, 442-450. 2008.
164. R Hashimoto, *et al.*: Pituitary adenylate cyclase-activating polypeptide is associated with schizophrenia. *Molecular Psychiatry* 12, 1026-1032. 2007.
165. Peter Holmans, *et al.*: Genetics of Recurrent Early-Onset Major Depression (GenRED): Final Genome Scan Report. *Am J Psychiatry* 164: 248-258. February 2007.
166. Kenneth, S: The Structure of Genetic and Environmental Risk Factors for Common Psychiatric and Substance Use Disorders in Men and Women. *Arch Gen Psychiatry* 60: 929-937. 2003.
167. Ma-Li Wong, *et al.*: Phosphodiesterase genes are associated with susceptibility to major depression and antidepressant treatment response. *PNAS* 10, vol 103: 41. 2006.
168. R Abou Jarma, *et al.*: Genetic variation of the FAT gene at 4q35 is associated with bipolar affective disorder. *Molecular Psychiatry* 13, 277-284. 2008.
169. Maynard, T M, Haskell, G T, Lieberman, J A, *et al.*: 22q11DS: genomic mechanisms and gene function in DiGeorge/velocardiofacialsyndrome. *International Journal of Developmental Neuroscience* 20, 407-419. 2002.
170. R J Cordery, *et al.*: *Journal of Neurology, Neurosurgery and Psychiatry* 76: 330-336. 2005.
171. N M Williams, *et al.*: *Schizophrenia Bulletin* 31 (4): 800-805. 2005.
172. Ustun, T B; Rehm, J, Chatterji, S, Saxena, S, Trotter, R, Room, R, Bickenbach, J, and the WHO/NIH Joint Project CAR Study Group: Multiple-informant ranking of the disabling effects of different health conditions in 14 countries. *The Lancet* 354 (9173): 111–115. 1999.
173. Goldberg, D P, *et al.*: *Manual of the General Health Questionnaire*. NFER Publishing, Windsor, England. 1978.
174. Goldberg, D P, Gater, R, Sartorius, N, Ustun, T B Piccinelli, M, Gureje, O, Rutter, C: The Validity of Two Versions of the GHQ in the WHO Study of Mental Illness in General Health Care. *Psychological Medicine* 27 (1):191-197. 1997.
175. Alonso, J, Angermeyer, MC, Bernert, S, Bruffaerts, R, *et al.*: 12-Month comorbidity patterns and associated factors in Europe: results from the European Study of the Epidemiology of Mental Disorders (ESEMeD) project. *Acta Psychiatr Scand Suppl*

420: 28-37. 2004.
176. K L Wisner, B L Parry, C M Piontek: Postpartum Depression. *N Engl J Med*, Vol 347, No 3: 194-199. 2002.
177. Lowe, B, Unutzer, J, Callahan, C M, Perkins, A J, Kroenke, K: Monitoring depression treatment outcomes with the patient health questionnaire –9. *Medical Care* 42 (12): 1194-1201. 2004.
178. Fearon, P, Kirkbride, J B, Dazzan, P, Morgan, C, Morgan, K, Lloyd, T, Hutchinson, G, Tarrant, J, Fung, W L A, Holloway, J, Mallett, R, Harrison, G, Leff, J, Jones, P B, Murray, R M: Incidence of schizophrenia and other psychoses in ethnic minority groups: results from the MRC AESOP Study. *Psychological Medicine* 26: 1-10. 2006.
179. J McGrath, S Saha, J Welham, *et al.*: A systematic review of the incidence of schizophrenia: the distribution of rates and the influence on sex, urbanity, migrant status and methodology. *BMC Medicine* 2: 13. 2004.
180. Oquendo, M A, *et al.*: Sex differences in clinical predictors of suicidal acts after major depression: a prospective study. *Am J Psychiatry* 164 (1):134-141. 2007.
181. Kessel, A S & Silverton, F: 'Ethics and Research in Psychiatry': In Prince, M, Stewart, R, Ford, T & Hotopf, M (eds): *Practical Psychiatric Epidemiology*. Oxford University Press. 2003.
182. Prince, M: 'Statistical methods in psychiatric epidemiology 2: an epidemiologist perspective'. In Prince, M, Stewart, R, Ford, T & Hotopf, M (eds): *Practical Psychiatric Epidemiology*. Oxford University Press. 2003.
183. Kaufman, Birmaher, Brent, Rao & Ryan: Diagnostic Interview Kiddie-Sads-Present and Lifetime Version (K-SADS-PL) Version 1.0 of October 1996.
184 Hassiotis, A, Strydom, A, Hall, I: Psychiatric morbidity and social functioning among adults with borderline intelligence living in private households. *Journal of Intellectual Disability Research*, Vol 52, No 2: pp 95-106 (12). February 2008.